Smart Collaboration for Lateral Hiring:

Successful strategies to recruit and integrate laterals in law firms

Authors
Dr Heidi K Gardner and Anusia E Gillespie

Managing director
Sian O'Neill

Smart Collaboration for Lateral Hiring: Successful Strategies to Recruit and Integrate Laterals in Law Firms
is published by

Globe Law and Business Ltd
3 Mylor Close, Horsell
Woking
Surrey GU21 4DD
United Kingdom
Tel: +44 20 3745 4770
www.globelawandbusiness.com

Smart Collaboration for Lateral Hiring: Successful Strategies to Recruit and Integrate Laterals in Law Firms

ISBN 9781787421967
EPUB ISBN 9781787421974
Adobe PDF ISBN 9781787421981
Mobi ISBN 9781787421998

Table of contents

List of figures and tables

I. Introduction:
Smart collaboration and lateral hiring

One of the biggest challenges in today's law firms is recruiting partners, experienced associates and senior business professionals into the firm – and then finding ways to integrate them, retain them and help make them sustainably productive. Firm leaders agree that the war for great talent is at least as brutal as the battle for clients. Yet many law firms mismanage and ultimately undervalue newly acquired talent because they do not have an actionable, data-driven strategy to help them flourish.

This special report offers a new, research-based approach for law firms to improve the lateral hiring of lawyers and business professionals, and the results. Our empirical studies demonstrate the clear benefits for lateral hires who engage in collaborative work with their new colleagues: retention and value production. Laterals who are deliberately integrated into the firm's existing client or internal work and supported in enticing peers to contribute to work they themselves have initiated are significantly more likely to stay with the firm longer, to hit or exceed their targets and to thrive professionally.

We call this kind of interactive work 'smart collaboration'.[1] Smart collaboration is essential to both the practice and business of law. It allows a team of talented problem solvers with specialised legal expertise to integrate their collective knowledge to tackle and solve their clients' thorniest problems, in ways that no single individual could accomplish. Similarly, experienced business professionals can combine their expertise with complementary others – for example, strategists collaborating with technologists and data analysts – to streamline and optimise organisational or client service processes.

While smart collaboration is critical to problem solving, how exactly does it improve lateral hiring outcomes? Smart collaboration helps firms to optimally use the collective expertise and experience of their newly hired members, which gives them the chance to start adding value early on. This in turn promotes their reputation and starts to foster others' trust in them. Collaboration also helps to bring lateral hires up to speed with the way the firm operates – especially the unwritten rules and cultural expectations that are hard to learn except through experience with people who know the norms. Further, it provides laterals with opportunities to build networks of colleagues who can enhance their work and for whom they can reciprocate by contributing valuable knowledge. Through these experiences, new joiners become part of the fabric of the firm, finding not only commercial and professional success, but also more meaning and deeper relationships. In short, smart collaboration – combined with clear planning and proper follow-through – can help lateral hires to acculturate and thrive. The trick, of course, is making sure that your firm is set up to foster this kind of lateral-incumbent collaboration.

For more than a decade, Dr Heidi K Gardner has been studying leadership, teamwork and talent development in professional service firms – first while on the faculty at Harvard Business School and now at Harvard Law School. She has amassed a database containing millions of timesheet, personnel and financial data records across dozens of law and other professional service firms; insights from hundreds of in-depth interviews with lawyers, business professionals, law firm leaders and clients; and responses from thousands of research surveys.

Anusia E Gillespie has been studying and immersed in the business of law for over 10 years in a variety of capacities, including practice and business roles at law firms and at Harvard Law School Executive Education. Attorney Gillespie collaborated with Dr Gardner to perform extensive research and interviews on lateral hiring in law firms in anticipation of this special report. The findings from the culmination of combined research are clear: lateral hiring integration and cross-disciplinary collaboration are essential to increase the odds that lateral hires will be successful and productive in their new firm.

This special report offers a clear rationale for altering your lateral hiring programme, while also providing the tools, processes and best practices for successful implementation. The research and findings are organised into four chapters:

- Chapter II outlines the rationale for change, including the ever-growing war for talent, the cost of losing laterals and the upsides of productive lateral hiring practices. This chapter emphasises why successful lateral hiring and integration are a business imperative in today's competitive marketplace.
- Chapter III offers a blueprint for law firms in determining how to assess and improve their current practices when hiring new talent. Each section relates to a specific phase of the hiring process (preparing to hire, recruiting and interviewing, and integration), with recommended actions and resource allocation, along with examples and case studies. Firms need a well-constructed plan, a relentless focus on execution and clear accountability if they expect to help laterals achieve two-way collaboration quickly and efficiently.
- Chapter IV wraps up the special report by synthesising the key messages, outlining some of the change management challenges associated with implementation and proposing a call to action.
- The appendix provides firms with practical, research-based tools, including an interview guide, best onboarding practices, new hire strategic considerations, a firm and client-based business plan, a logic-driven decision tree, database criteria for assessing new hiring practices from the last five years and case studies for comparative analysis.

Productive lateral hiring has the power to grow revenues, increase innovation and build an inclusive firm culture. In fact, a typical firm spends roughly 70% of total expenses on talent, including recruitment, salaries, benefits, training and retention. But firms often fail to create intentional processes – onboarding, collaboration and long-term integration that evolves with the needs of the hire – to provide new laterals with the smoothest transition. Going forward, firms will need to allocate significant funds to cybersecurity and other technology investments just to stay alive. Those that fix and optimise their talent systems to save money will maintain profitability; others risk a downward spiral of lower profits, then loss of exceptional talent, which further reduces profitability. If your firm is failing to fully harness the power of your talent, the time for research-based strategic change is now.

"You need talent not only with the right expertise, but also with the willingness to use knowledge in a collaborative way to tackle clients' and your firm's most complicated, high-value problems and opportunities."

II. The business case for integrating lateral hires

1. The war for talent
Law firms' war for talent is rooted in their war for clients. Increasingly, sophisticated clients are demanding much more from their law firms, including cross-disciplinary problem solving that draws on expertise in law, business, technology and strategy. One-dimensional legal problems have swelled into multi-faceted business problems that span departments, disciplines and geographies. As one general counsel put it, "I don't have legal problems. I have 'problem' problems."

Moreover, regulatory changes have opened the door to increased competition from new players in the legal arena. The focus on quality metrics and output-based performance measures is upending traditional ways of measuring work. Clients are demanding diverse teams because they know that diversity promotes innovation and superior quality. Technology is driving down costs and creating both opportunities and threats for many kinds of legal working. As a result, law firms are facing the urgent question of how to adapt to a globalised legal marketplace in the midst of disruption and reinvention.

The only sustainable way to respond is to make sure you have talent not only with the right expertise, but also with the willingness to use knowledge in a collaborative way to tackle clients' and your firm's most complicated, high-value problems and opportunities. The firms that will thrive in this hyper-competitive, dynamic market are those which have figured out what mix of talent they need to achieve their strategy – and which know that mix includes more than the most senior lawyers. Strategically minded firms are seeking strong business professionals: leaders with few (if any) client-facing responsibilities who focus on the successful operation of the firm in core functions such as marketing, finance, IT and human resources. Talented executives streamline processes to help lawyers focus on the 'bread and butter' of the firm. The best business professionals are therefore just as critical to firm profitability and success as their legal counterparts.

Law firms are therefore fighting a war for talent on three fronts: for partners, for more junior lawyers and for business professionals. And for each segment, this war is hotter than ever.

For partners, increased mobility has fostered the emergence of a free-agent mentality. Encouraged by growing legions of headhunters, experienced legal practitioners today have a keen sense of their value in the marketplace and face far fewer cultural taboos about jumping ship for a more lucrative offer. In some of the hottest areas, it is not unusual for professionals with an in-demand specialty to receive multiple calls every week from recruiters or competitors jockeying for their expertise.

Similarly, high-performing associates are also experiencing a jump in desirability. As firms expand their reach – in terms of both industries and jurisdictions – they are seeking 'up-and-comers' who view switching firms as a strategy for achieving higher compensation and quicker promotion to partner. For millennial associates, switching firms is commonplace, as they never experienced the stigma that plagued older generations. "An expanded network, a signing bonus and a shorter runway to partner if I play my cards right," said one associate in our research about the potential benefits of switching firms. "I like my current firm, but I would be crazy not to make a move soon."

Layered on top of this is the breakdown of the former gentlemen's agreements that divided up the legal landscape into what might be called 'spheres of influence'. In the legal field – as in many other professional fields, including accounting, engineering and consulting – the entrance of international firms into previously domestic markets has fuelled competition for top-end partners. For example, when US firms began their push into London, many City lawyers massively spiked their income by joining the first wave of partners to sign up with these newcomer firms.

This trend transcends even formerly stable localised markets such as

Bogota, Munich, Phoenix and scores of other cities around the world. For example, when firms such as DLA Piper and CMS expand their Latin American presence, their arrival causes a significant uptick in labour market competition – not only for partners, but also for associates. Tales abound of lawyers doubling their salaries overnight and then subsequently negotiating for additional perks such as preferred parking, flexitime and increased holidays.

In many jurisdictions, a 'new normal' has emerged concerning salaries and poaching. Many Chilean law firms have reportedly skipped over their direct competitors by recruiting lawyers from in-house positions into a range of practice areas. Full-scale lift-outs of entire practice groups are likely to become the next phase for recruiting in these hot legal markets. Yet the odds of success for all these lateral hiring efforts is worse than a coin toss.

So far, we have hinted at the idea that collaboration plays a critical role in changing the success equation, and we return to that idea more fully towards the end of this chapter. First, though, we consider what is at stake if your firm does not take steps to drastically increase the likelihood of success in lateral hiring.

2. The cost of losing laterals

Laterals – partners, associates and business professionals – who leave the firm significantly depress the bottom line. While firms fiercely compete to recruit and hire the industry's best and brightest, accumulating stars without a strategic plan and simply hoping for the best does not work. Most firms recognise – and research confirms – that it takes three to five years for star lateral hires just to reach the level of performance they achieved in their old firms, let alone to become even more productive.[2]

In reality, though, most lateral hires who are struggling to become productive in their new firm simply don't push through the 'pain barrier' and stay long enough to reach previous levels of stardom. Instead, they leave the firm after a few years, at best. And for all failed lateral hires, it is not just their expertise that walks out the door. The critical relationships that they had curated internally and externally to problem solve and produce – these also disappear.[3]

2.1 Lateral partners

In law firms, the area that is most researched is that of lateral partner productivity and retention. One study of leading law firms in London yielded some truly abysmal statistics: fully 20% of lateral partners were no longer with the firm one year after joining and 50% had left within five years.[4] The latter figure corresponds to a recent study of the global legal market, showing that the average five-year attrition rate for lateral partners is an astounding 47%.[5] **Research in labour economics suggests that the cost of each failed lateral partner is more than double the individual's annual compensation – 213%, to be precise.**[6] So, for example, the typical cost of replacing an equity partner in the United Kingdom will be at least £500,000; for equity partners in top firms, however, that cost rises to a staggering £3.3 million.[7] When considering the cost of failed hires, firms may calculate the direct costs (eg, recruiter fees, bonus guarantees); but many fail to appreciate indirect costs such as the opportunity costs of partners' time spent interviewing.

Given that two to three years of strong performance are needed to recoup recruiting costs and compensation-above-contribution through the transition period, the attrition of lateral partners at five years is a loss-making proposition for most law firms today.

Beyond failing to retain star lateral partners, firms typically have another cohort of under-performing lateral partners who do stay at the firm, but fail to achieve a profitable return on investment. The Wharton School's Matthew Bidwell, in a study of lateral hiring aptly named "Paying More to Get Less", looked at six years of personnel data from the US investment banking branch of a financial services

Figure 1. Regional averages of five-year lateral partner attrition rates

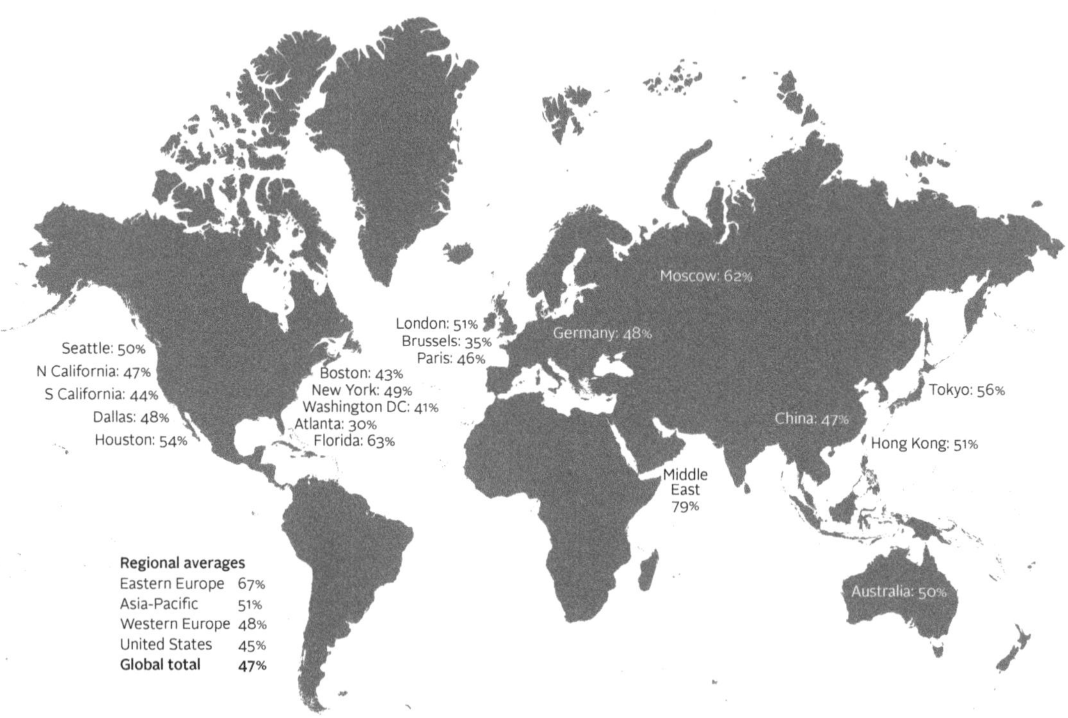

Source: Hugh A Simons, "Global Lateral Hiring by The Numbers: A Look Behind the High 5-Year Attrition Rate", The American Lawyer International, *3 February 2017*

corporation. He found that, despite external hires generally having more education and experience than internal hires, external hires performed significantly worse for the first two years of their employment than workers who were promoted to the same job from within the organisation. Furthermore, he discovered that lateral hires were far more likely than internal workers to leave their job – because they either quit or were fired. At the same time, Bidwell concluded, external hires cost the firm 18% more money in salaries than did their internally promoted colleagues.[8]

Most law firm leaders we interviewed believe that a similar pattern holds across the legal sector. As one partner explained, "Failures linger longer in many firms: the longer they stay, the more problematic. Most firms fail to recognise or lack a mechanism to deal with the problem of an unproductive lateral. So many firms have favourable policies under their partnership agreement that make it really hard to get rid of disasters."

In addition to recruiting and compensation costs, lateral partners may consume resources that firms are unable to recoup. For example, if expectations are not properly managed, a lateral partner who was previously employed at a firm with a heavy business development focus may unintentionally blow the new firm's marketing budget by filling an active conference calendar.

Overview of costs for sub-par lateral hiring

- Financial: £500,000-£3 million+
- Underperformers who stay and fail to become productive
- Weakened or damaged organisational culture
- Stress on internal resources (ex marketing budgets).
- Internal friction related to unequal compensation
- Weakened client confidence

Lateral partner hiring can also cause internal strife about the compensation system among long-term partners because firms generally need to pay much more for individuals brought in from outside in order to compensate them for the risk of changing firms. In US law firms, for example, the pressures associated with lateral partner hiring can lead to significant disparities in compensation between partners within the same firm. Although the median spread between the highest and lowest-paid partners inside a US firm is 10:1 (already quite a gap), that ratio swells as high as a staggering 23:1 in one firm where lateral hiring is rampant.

Another major risk associated with hiring lateral talent might be the dilution – or worse – of a firm's culture. Sometimes adding employees

"If you do these types of things to integrate business professionals, you're going to create and foster the environment that you want within your team: less drama, people paying attention to performance, and doing what they need to get things done. You'll have lower turnover rates, and fewer people calling out at the last minute because they are ill and needed a break. We've seen it happen."

Chief talent officer, AmLaw100 firm

with different perspectives can benefit firms by introducing new ways of thinking. But unless you are deliberately seeking and hiring candidates with a specific, diverse set of characteristics, you are leaving the evolution of your culture to chance by hiring people who come from firms with cultures that are radically different from your own.

A final cost to mention, which is difficult to quantify but nevertheless significant, is client confidence. Once a client has confidence that a trusted lawyer is invested in its particular business matter, the departure of that partner can be devastating to the trust between firm and client. An ever-changing roster conjures unfavourable questions in the client's mind: "If this firm can't handle its personnel, how can it effectively solve my high-stakes problem?"

2.2 Business professionals and associates

Law firms face significant costs related to poor outcomes for both laterally hired business professionals and associates. The Society for Strategic Human Resource Management estimates that the cost of replacing a skilled business professional ranges from six to nine months' salary; replacing an average-paid chief marketing officer (CMO) in a typical US law firm, for example, would therefore cost between $200,000 and $400,000.[9] The cost of replacing an associate is similar: estimates range from $200,000 to $500,000, and this figure does not account for 'hidden' costs such as client dissatisfaction related to service team churn or damage to attorney morale.[10] This adds up to significant firm-wide expense. Turnover costs can represent more than 12% of pre-tax income for the average company; and for those with higher-than-average turnover (which is the case at most law firms), costs can be nearly 40% of earnings.[11]

In addition to direct financial costs in the turnover of business professionals, there are culture and client costs. Consider an executive example: the CMO. CMO turnover is an issue for corporations and professional service firms alike; one article dubbed the phenomenon the "disposable CMO".[12] While we do not have statistics specific to CMO turnover in law firms, a recent law firm survey of CMO tenure illustrates the point: 53% of responding CMOs had been with their firms for five years or less, with 32% reporting a tenure of three years or less (see Figure 2).[13] This turnover leads to instability in the firm's entire marketing department. The remaining business professionals experience the stress and concern related to the unknown: "Who will be my new boss? What is their management and leadership style? Will I still be able to work on the projects I am enjoying now?" CMO turnover can also result in inconsistencies in the firm's brand strategy,

Figure 2. CMO tenure from 2017 report based on US, Canada and UK sample set

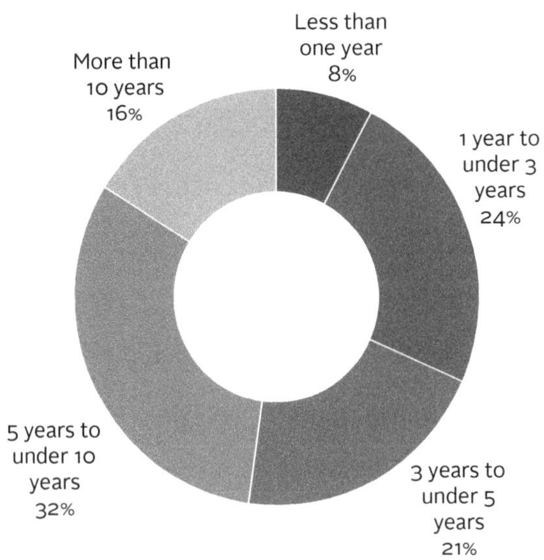

Source: Calibrate Legal, Law Firm Marketing Operations Index

client relationship management activities and client-facing marketing programmes; and nowadays, with CMOs becoming increasingly involved in service delivery, it can negatively affect client satisfaction.[14] As mid-sized firms fight to increase business generation to avoid acquisition and large firms grip tightly onto their brand prestige and recognition, this type of turnover is a risky proposition in the changing legal market, which is starting to feel like quicksand.

The financial costs of losing and replacing associates are lower than those for partners and will of course vary from firm to firm (see the Appendix for a diagnostic tool to determine your costs). While firms may not experience all of the non-financial costs associated with partner turnover – the underperformance costs, large draws on internal resources (associates require approvals) or internal friction related to unequal compensation (associates will not have access to this data) – all firms will 'feel the pain' around maintaining the morale and productivity of remaining associates in an environment of high associate turnover. Depending on the seniority of the departing associate(s), firms may also experience a decline in client confidence – another whack on client loyalty and business generation that firms simply cannot afford in today's market.

"At far too many law firms, exceptional CMOs, CHROs, COOs and other leaders find themselves underutilised and undervalued because of their 'non-lawyer' status. The legal industry needs to get past this outdated idea. Far from being 'overheads', these business service leaders play an essential role in the firm's success by enabling revenue production and growth."

Jennifer Scalzi, CEO of Calibrate Legal

3. The threat and impact of new competition for lateral hires
Today's law firms are operating in a highly transparent labour market. Professionals are candidly talking to one another, across disciplines and across professions, to compare notes on career opportunities. Job websites such as Glassdoor and Indeed reveal anonymous insider information about a firm, cultural norms and compensation. Consequently, law firms are finding that the playing field for the war for talent is quickly expanding, requiring firms to investigate what other organisations are offering to attract new talent.

A straightforward, effective method for collecting that data is to perform exit interviews with employees to learn about the organisations that have lured them away. An exit interview provides the best opportunity to gather transparent and direct feedback that a current employee may be unwilling to share. You need to gather these insights to figure out how you can best compete in the lateral market.

Competition is no longer limited to other law firms or even in-house legal departments. Law firm talent is being lured to late-stage start-ups with a culture that millennials in particular perceive as more authentic, dynamic and interesting. Premier professional service firms such as McKinsey are highly attractive for associates – and increasingly even partners – who want to build their business skills and learn best practices. Big Four accounting firms, such as PwC, are also a threat. These firms are beginning to compete directly with law firms – even in the highly regulated US market, as evidenced by PwC's opening of a law firm in Washington DC in 2017.[15] These accounting firms need lawyers to build out their newfound legal practices and business professionals who understand the law firm market to adequately compete – and the plan is to poach this talent from your law firms.

Corporate legal departments are also seizing the opportunity to acquire and retain the best legal talent. One commentator explained it this way:[16] "General counsel will increasingly operate ambidextrously: taking work from Big Law to execute in-house with one hand, while outsourcing work currently executed in-house to outsourced service providers with the other. This is a once-in-a-career moment for forward-thinking general counsel: push less interesting work out, take more interesting work in and earn plaudits from management for lowering the company's overall legal cost."

Increasingly, leaders of in-house legal departments are making public and explicit their goals to poach talent. One general counsel of a high-tech company told students during a panel at Harvard Law School: "I am keeping the sexiest work in-house because I want to tell recruits that they will do the most cutting-edge work by joining us. Silicon Valley is a brutal labour market and the best way to attract hot legal talent is by promising them that they will tackle sophisticated, pioneering problems – which are exactly the kind that used to get farmed out to external law firms. Not any more."

It's about the work for business professionals, too. They are increasingly demanding, and deserving of, a prominent voice in the business of law. Savvy business professionals who are not integrated into the core of the law firm – executive committee included – will find positions where the question of whether they 'have a seat at the table' is never considered, because it is so engrained as a given. As advanced business professionals continue to carve out professional opportunities in new and interesting ways, the heat is on law firms to convince candidates that they will be trusted to do their jobs, without micro-management from lawyers.

4. Smart collaboration for lateral hires' success

Firms have historically sought lateral talent to help bolster their prestige and fill unmet needs to serve growing practice areas. Today, firms are laser focused on an additional objective: problem-solving power. Lateral hires are a hot commodity because cross-disciplinary expertise is essential to help both the most lucrative clients to tackle their thorniest problems and the law firm itself to navigate and remain competitive in the constantly evolving legal market. In other words, while lawyers must collaborate and create diverse teams to solve complex problems for their clients, law firm business professionals must do the same for their client: the law firm.

How did we move from building out practice areas to curating both legal and business cross-disciplinary bench strength? As law firms and their clients continue to globalise, their problems have become – to borrow a term from business – 'VUCA' (volatile, uncertain, complex and ambiguous). These problems transcend traditional disciplinary silos and require coordinated teams of experts to solve them – they require collaboration. **How can firms ensure that their lawyers collaborate effectively to solve complex client issues, and that their business professionals collaborate to most effectively tackle their strategic objectives in this rapidly changing market? Institutionalising collaboration must happen early and often – and that starts with integrating your new lateral hires.**

Given that only about 24% of US organisations of all sizes and industries have successful integration practices – a figure significantly lower in law firms – this area represents the proverbial 'low-hanging fruit'.[17] Firms that optimise lateral onboarding and integration enjoy significant long-term benefits, including increased revenue, stronger and more diverse teams, a tight-knit culture and a growing network that creates unforeseen and welcome business opportunities.

Numerous studies agree: proactive, comprehensive integration increases job satisfaction, expedites individual productivity, facilitates collaboration with others and more easily promotes an inclusive culture.[18]

To reap the benefits of a long-time, productive lateral-hire employee, firms must invest in new hires early on. Approximately 90% of new hires use the first six months of employment to decide whether they want to continue their employment.[19] For lateral partners, our analysis shows that they must be sufficiently integrated with incumbent partners and clients within the first 18 months, if not sooner, to succeed at the firm. Specifically, two things need to happen in that short time: lateral partners need to have the opportunity to work with at least a couple of the firm's incumbent clients (on pitches, if not actual projects), and they need a couple of long-term partners to help on the client work they generate (either clients they have imported or new clients). That is, firms need to encourage laterals to collaborate both ways: receive and give referrals on substantive client work. If either is missing, new lateral partners are at a higher risk of leaving; if neither happens, they are very likely to leave the firm by their three-year anniversary,[20] as illustrated in Figure 3.

Figure 3. The collaboration required to retain lateral partners

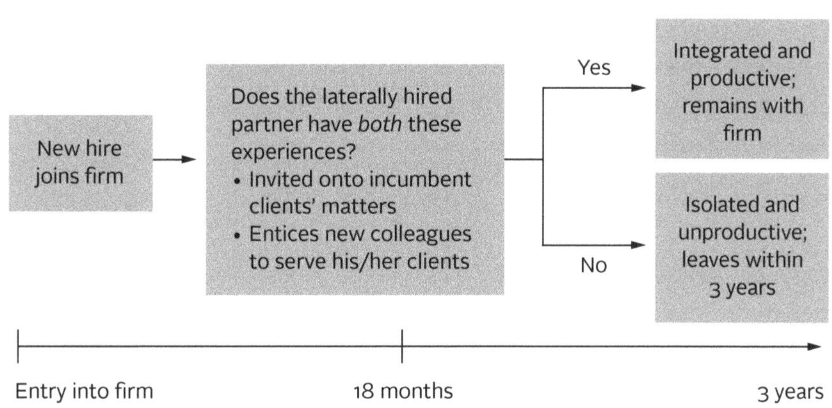

Source: Dr Heidi K Gardner

The conundrum for lateral partners, however, is that most firms train lawyers as subject-matter specialists. Because most top-tier law firms understand that their clients increasingly expect each of their lawyers to be the foremost expert in a specific domain, firms have fostered expertise specialisation by creating narrowly defined practice areas and by rewarding professionals for developing reputations in precise niches. The collective expertise has therefore become distributed across people, places and practice groups. Consequently, tackling client problems that transcend practice areas and disciplinary silos seriously challenges traditional models of law firm structure and ways of doing business.

Professor Rob Cross applies social network theory to study how organisational investments can more productively create and leverage internal and external employee networks.[21] Perhaps counterintuitively, one significant insight from Cross's work is that bigger networks are not necessarily better.[22] In fact, they often relate to high turnover, either because new hires waste time building connections with people who are ultimately not useful in their roles or because they inadvertently breed mistrust by continuously talking about how they used their expertise for their prior employer. We hear that many law firms use 'speed dating' sessions to introduce newcomers into the firm, but Cross's research shows that these sessions could actually backfire unless they are carefully orchestrated.

Clearly, firms need a well-constructed plan, a relentless focus on execution and clear accountability processes if they expect to help laterals achieve two-way collaboration quickly and efficiently. To keep up, law firms must properly hire and integrate lateral talent to ensure that the lateral becomes embedded in cross-disciplinary teams – that is, to ensure collaboration. Firms that implement the strategic processes outlined in this special report will increase the chances of productive lateral hiring and reap the myriad benefits of retaining their sought-after talent.

III. The three-stage process for successful lateral hiring

Assuming that your firm concludes that the potential upsides to hiring laterals outweigh the downsides, you can better your odds with laterals by following these critical action steps. They fall into three phases:

- Stage 1: preparing to hire;
- Stage 2: recruiting and interviewing; and
- Stage 3: integration

Our research indicates that firms currently spend about 15% of time on Stage 1, 80% on Stage 2 and only 5% on Stage 3. To make lateral hiring a success, firms need to spread their efforts more evenly across the three phases. By spending additional time on Stages 1 and 3, firms can capture hidden value – directly improving the bottom line.

As shown in Figure 4, firms need to spend about 267% *more* time on preparing to hire, 62.5% *less* time on recruitment and **600% more time on integrating lateral hires**. To bring this home, consider that you currently spend 60 hours on hiring a lateral – that is, nine hours on Stage 1, 48 hours on Stage 2 and a mere three hours on Stage 3. A shift to best practices would require spending 24 hours thoughtfully preparing to hire, 18 hours recruiting and interviewing, and another 18 hours on properly integrating your lateral into the fabric of the firm.

Figure 4. Allocation of time spent on each stage of the lateral hiring process

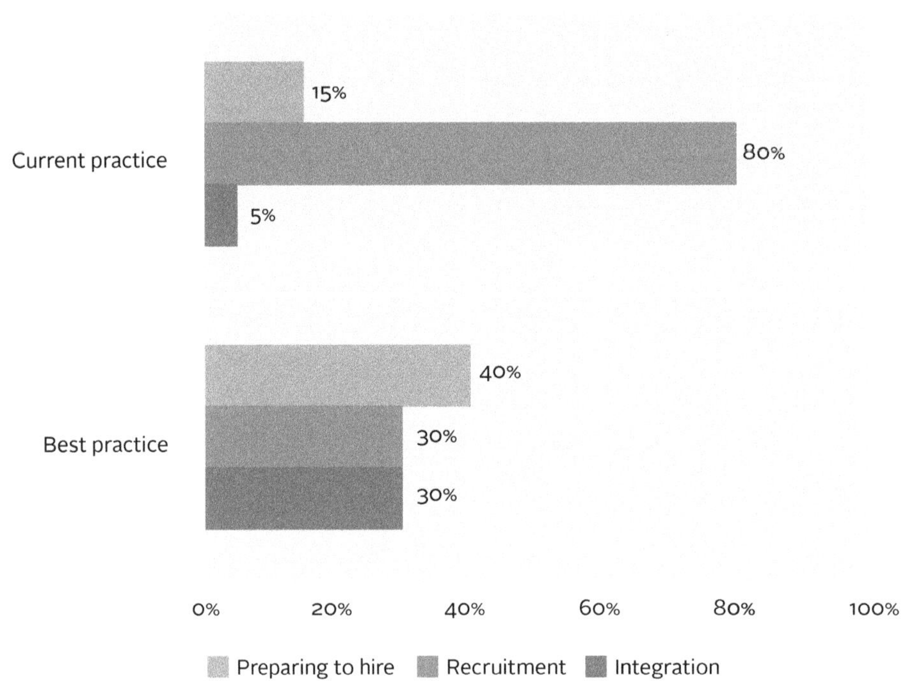

Source: Dr Heidi K Gardner and Anusia E Gillespie

We offer a roadmap to achieve this 40/30/30 split, thereby spending your time and energy on the right things for the right amount of time, and ultimately improving the success of your firm's lateral hiring. Table 1 details the best practices of each of the three hiring phases. Let us now consider each in turn.

1. Stage 1: preparing to hire

1.1 Connect your talent plan to the firm's strategic plan

Strategy defines how an organisation will attempt to achieve sustainable competitive advantage by preserving what is distinctive about the company – either by performing different activities from rivals or by performing similar activities differently.[23] Strategy "bridges the chasm between vision and tactics".[24] Strategy requires making tough choices about what a firm wants to be known for, where it should invest and where it should refrain from 'playing'. Once a firm has set its overall strategy, every sub-unit, department and practice group should build its strategy to best support the overarching goals. A firm that achieves this is said to be in 'alignment', where efforts and efficiencies are maximised in pursuit of the highest goals of the firm.[25]

The very best professional service firms are well aligned, with few problems of strategic hiring and retention. For most law firms,

Table 1. The three-stage process to successful lateral hiring in law firms

Stage 1 **Preparing to hire** **(40% of time)**	**Stage 2** **Recruitment** **(30% of time)**	**Stage 3** **Integration** **(30% of time)**
Best Practices		
1.1 Connect your talent plan to the firm's strategic plan. *Chapter III, section 1.1.* 1.2 Update analysis of future needs. *See Chapter III, section 1.2.* 1.3 Define the expertise needed and think creatively about the professionals who are best placed to meet objectives. *See Chapter III, section 1.3.* 1.4 Consider internal 'laterals' before looking for external candidates. *See Chapter III, section 1.4.* 1.5 Create a data-driven business plan. *See Chapter III, section 1.5.* 1.6 Run analyses to track pockets of 'churn and burn'. *See Chapter III, section 1.6.* 1.7 Define the role and articulate the required capabilities. *See Chapter III, section 1.7.* 1.8 Develop the talent pool. *See Chapter III, section 1.8.* 1.9 Allocate the support necessary for success. *See Chapter III, section 1.9.*	2.1 Search for capabilities over credentials. *See Chapter III, section 2.1.* 2.2 Evaluate candidates for technical and leadership competence, collaborative capacity, cultural fit and firm experience. *See Chapter III, section 2.2.* 2.3 Identify and train the right group of people to conduct interviews using structured interviews with behavioural-based questions. *See Chapter III, section 2.3.* 2.4 Determine key qualifications and assign scores to each. *See Chapter III, section 2.4.* 2.5 Use the interview data to debrief and make decisions. *See Chapter III, section 2.5.* 2.6 Close the deal. *See Chapter III, section 2.6.*	3.1 Make laterals' experience meaningful from Day 1 and start even before they officially join. *See Chapter III, section 3.1.* 3.2 Acquaint with the culture and shape processes around new hires' strengths. *See Chapter III, section 3.2.* 3.3 Assign a peer mentor. *See Chapter III, section 3.3.* 3.4 Assist new joiners in building their networks. *See Chapter III, section 3.4.* 3.5 Hold new joiners, the hiring partner and peers accountable for success. *See Chapter III, section 3.5.* 3.6 Continuously audit and revamp the lateral integration process. *See Chapter III, section 3.6.*

Source: Dr Heidi K Gardner and Anusia E Gillespie

however, hiring is more akin to a fire drill than a deliberate process, which leads to the kinds of costs and missed opportunities discussed in the previous chapter. How can you change that?

The critical first step is to identify the multiple firm-specific goals that can and should be addressed during the hiring process. The firm must be thoughtful about its strategy to avoid a dilutive 'best at everything' approach. Instead, the firm should decide on three to five of the most important goals connected to its talent strategy and explicitly connect the firm objectives with talent tactics.[26]

Clearly, every firm will have different objectives given its size, maturity and growth stage. Consider, for example, a firm that has identified the following three strategic goals which could be supported with a clear talent acquisition and retention plan:

- Create strong relationships among colleagues;
- Diversify the firm's talent pool; and
- Enhance the firm's reputation.

The firm decided to connect these goals to talent for specific reasons. First, the firm has found that individuals who have strong networks within the firm are more likely to succeed in its 'up or out' promotion system. Second, the firm is based in the United States, where clients (especially federal and state governments, but also public corporations) are demanding that their service providers employ a greater proportion of women and racial minorities. Third, in the increasingly competitive legal market, the firm wants to ensure the strength of its reputation not only for high-quality work, but also as a good place to work with smart management. The firm understands that its reputation is built and sustained based primarily on the quality of its people, and that the rigour and tact of the hiring process – including leaving those who do not receive an offer with a positive impression – send a strong signal to the market about how seriously the firm manages this critical asset. Table 2 explicitly connects these firm-level strategic objectives with select talent tactics in the preparing to hire stage. This exercise can and should be performed for every action in your firm's lateral hiring process.

1.2 Update analysis of future needs

Firms should continuously assess their current pipeline against anticipated needs to inform the firm's evolving talent plan. The firm's lateral hiring strategy should be a direct outgrowth of this ever-evolving plan.

In our research, however, we found that firms typically hire in a 'plug and play' fashion. In hiring lateral lawyers, firms tend to fill a perceived

Table 2. Connecting the firm's talent strategy to its strategic objectives

Multiple firm-specific strategic objectives				
	Actions	**1. Relationships**	**2. Diversity**	**3. Reputation**
Preparing to hire	**Articulate capabilities needed**	Incumbents are more likely to support and want to work with colleagues who are meeting expectations for the role.	Delineating specific capabilities to hire for opens the candidate pool beyond specific credentials or backgrounds and deters 'mini-me' hiring.	Being 'on the same page' with candidates about what capabilities are required for the job increases the likelihood that candidates will feel the ultimate decision was fair.
	Determine what type of expert you need – not necessarily a lawyer	X	Out-of-the-box thinking as to how best to fulfil service needs allows consideration of a broader variety of experts, and therefore more diverse talent.	The firm is viewed as thoughtful and progressive in its hiring decisions to best serve clients, and the brand is exposed to more markets.
	Engage your workforce to develop the talent pool	Incentivising employees to proactively reach out to their networks, announce openings on social media and otherwise tap into their networks creates a team-effort mentality that deepens intra-firm relationships.	Draws on more perspectives on the ideal candidate than those in the recruiting group and attracts different audiences with customised messaging.	Signals enthusiasm about the firm and the position, increases brand exposure and presents the firm as a savvy consumer of talent.

Source: Dr Heidi K Gardner and Anusia E Gillespie, adapted from Heidi K Gardner, Hiring Successful Professionals: One Process – Multiple Goals *(Harvard Business School, July 2010)*

"We're morphing into hiring more strategically and connecting new hires to the broader goals and needs of the organisation, both in the immediate time period as well as one year, two years, three years down the road. But I still think we just aren't as sophisticated as some of our corporate clients."

Chief talent officer, global law firm

gap either when a lawyer leaves the firm or when there is an uptick in work for a particular practice area. Both approaches are reactive in nature. Similarly, we found that most firms have a purely reactive strategy when hiring for business professionals – someone leaves, the job description gets posted, the recruiter is engaged and the search is on. These kinds of hiring strategies are based on past needs. In a mature organisation operating in a stagnant market and in maintenance mode, these kinds of hiring practices may be the right fit. However, for **law firms fighting for clients and talent in an increasingly globalised marketplace with shifting regulations and the constant threat of disruption, a hiring strategy based on past or in-demand needs will not allow you to move quickly enough to outpace the competition.**

How can you excel in this area? Firms must review their talent requirements at least once a year and develop dynamic succession plans for top performers throughout the organisation, not just the managing partners. Sophisticated firms deepen client relationships by establishing a team of specialists, in conjunction with the originating partner, to seamlessly and effectively engage, manage and (later) transition client work. 'Laddering' – a term used to describe the approach of matching attorneys on the client service team with similarly tenured in-house lawyers at the client for mutual learning and relationship building – is a powerful strategy that helps firms to maintain a steady stream of talent at all levels and take over the client relationship as time progresses by putting in place an organic client succession structure. Our research reveals that collaborative teams within that framework promote firm inclusivity, employee retention and client satisfaction. Most importantly, teams as part of a dynamic succession plan highlight future talent needs more quickly and proactively.

Firms should intentionally discuss client transition and retirement plans early on – a good marker is five years post-partnership – to increase the likelihood of a smooth transition and eliminate any stigma associated with passing key clients to the next generation of vibrant talent. These meetings provide partners with the opportunity to articulate their deep-seeded career aspirations and allow firms to strategically assist them in achieving those goals. Time also allows the firm to carefully craft how to transition client work and provides clients with the opportunity to give input.

Firms should also create and maintain databases that combine information from various talent pipeline sources, such as internal mobility, employee referral programmes (if your firm does not have one, consider its implementation), and external recruiting yields, along with predictions on future business needs and talent attrition rates. The benefits of investing the resources to create such a system

Figure 5. Forecasting talent needs

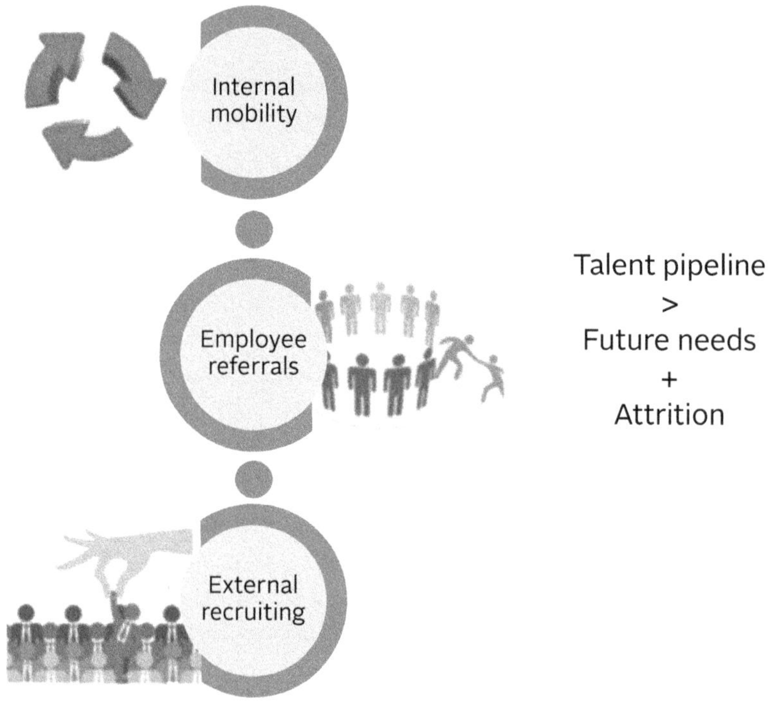

Source: Dr Heidi K Gardner and Anusia E Gillespie

include the reduced risk of expertise gaps in the face of client demands, more strategic hiring, improved budgeting and a smoother experience for the laterals themselves. As proof of the same, consider US-based software company Intuit, which built a proprietary system combining talent pipeline data and business forecasting that has allowed it to predict 90% of its talent needs, thereby reducing its recruiting, attrition and integration costs.[27]

1.3 Define the expertise needed and think creatively about who is best placed to meet objectives

Firms need to have the right people in the right positions performing the right functions, and in this market that means addressing the right questions, such as the following:

- What function do we need to meet our objectives?
- How do we position that function within the firm?
- What are the skills and expertise needed to succeed in that position?
- Do those include being a lawyer?

Perhaps the expertise needed for a professional position does include being a trained lawyer. But the flipside is also true: perhaps the firm thinks it needs to hire a lawyer when in fact a highly skilled businessperson in the technology sector, for instance, would better align with the position objectives.

As the general counsel of a Fortune 100 company explains, "Despite what they think, most individual lawyers are actually quite replaceable. I mean, I could find a decent tax lawyer in most firms. But when that lawyer teamed up with colleagues from IP, regulatory and ultimately litigation, I couldn't find a whole-team substitute in another firm." Taking that one step further, when your firm embraces collaboration among its lawyers and other professionals, that allows you to embrace even more complex client needs.

In addition to cross-practice collaboration of firm partners and associates to create and deliver advice customised to client industry, firms are beginning to collaborate more heavily with sophisticated business professionals on the marketing, business and client development teams. Increasingly, general counsel expect outside lawyers to provide not just more holistic solutions, but holistic solutions that are customised and tailored to the client's industry. They care about this sector-specific tailoring for reasons along a continuum that ranges from highly substantive to more symbolic customisation, as depicted in Figure 6.

Figure 6. The types of legal service customisation that clients demand

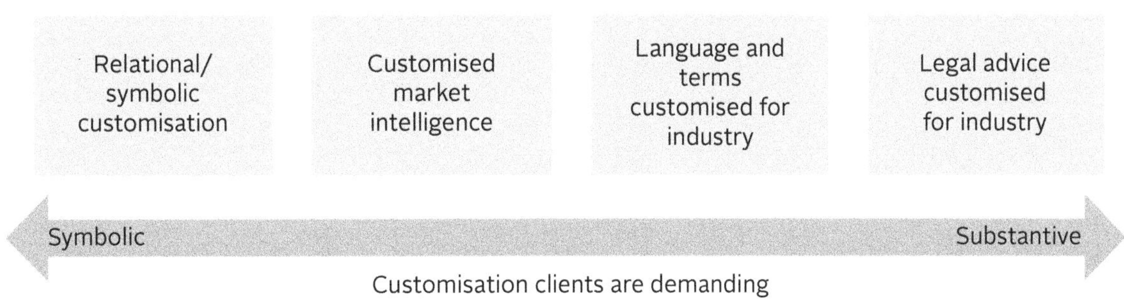

Source: Dr Heidi K Gardner and Anusia E Gillespie

Table 3. Descriptions of the types of customisation that clients demand

Type of customisation	Description of customisation	Opportunity for lawyers and other professionals to collaborate?
Relational/ symbolic	At one end of the spectrum is customisation that may not be strictly necessary on a content basis, but is important to general counsel because it indicates that their external law firm values them as a client and is willing to take the extra steps to provide them with advice that is not generic. This represents a signalling or symbolic value to customisation.	Yes – for example, a business development professional could digest a recent white paper and provide it to a lawyer to send to a client with two or three sentences on why the client should care and what the implications are for the client.
Market intelligence	One general counsel said to us: "If my outside lawyer can tell me just one thing that my competitors are doing better than I am, I'd give them all the time in the world." Obviously, we can speak at length about the related ethics and confidentiality, but that kind of market intelligence is tremendously important to clients and simultaneously very difficult for general counsel to gather. And it is often something that lawyers should have ready access to, if they are operating in a big enough firm and collaborating with their colleagues. This all leads to the idea of collaboration in the sense that an industry sector is a natural place for lawyers inside a law firm, who have different specialisations, to come together, share their understanding of both the substance and the trends, and develop ways to provide higher-value services to the client.	Yes – for example, a business professional with training on the forces that shape industry trends and who sits at the intersection of various practice groups or leads a sector group should regularly engage attorneys in insight-generating training, and then package those insights for existing and prospective clients.

Source: Dr Heidi K Gardner and Anusia E Gillespie

continued on next page

Type of customisation	Description of customisation	Opportunity for lawyers and other professionals to collaborate?
Language and terms	Further along,there is a more substantive reason for customisation related to terminology. For example, we had an interview with a life sciences client who complained that his outside counsel repeatedly gave him advice that he could not use directly with his own internal clients. His internal clients were PhD and physician-PhD executives who expected people to speak their language. But the general counsel was constantly put in the position of translating the advice from his outside counsel – a time-consuming and laborious process. This type of customisation along the lines of jargon or terminology makes legal advice more applicable and user friendly.	Yes – for example, technical medical experts in a firm specialising in intellectual property should consistently review legal documents and lawyer communications to ensure that the content is appropriately translated for the general counsel's internal clients.
Legal advice	Clients are increasingly asking for customised approaches because the actual content of the legal advice they are seeking must be tailored to that specific industry. Data privacy, for example, means something very different to a hospital client than it does to a retail client or to a financial institution. And although there is a body of knowledge that is generalisable, the way that knowledge gets applied is very different from industry to industry and, therefore, clients are asking for their advice to be customised for substantive reasons.	Yes – opportunity for technology-enabled collaboration. Opportunity for lawyers and business professionals to collaborate on technical legal advice is limited; but with advances in technology, lawyers will likely be working with artificial intelligence or other technology to deliver customised legal advice.

Accordingly, if industry customisation is part of the firm's overall strategy, the firm must consider the appropriate talent to fill gaps in industry service. Does the firm need niche industry expertise in the form of legal advice or business orientation? If the latter, the firm might be best served by hiring a business-savvy professional instead of another partner. Or, as we discuss immediately below, the best option might be to source internal candidates who are looking for this kind of position.

1.4 Consider internal 'laterals' before looking for external candidates

Given the research cited above on the relative success rate and costs of internal versus external hires, you need to analyse your firm's current capacity and utilisation to reveal whether your market needs can be covered by an existing internal resource. Set the bar high to convince yourself that a lateral is the only option.

As the chief operations officer (COO) of a US-based consulting firm phrased it:

> *In at least 80% of the cases where a partner requests a lateral hire, our analysis of staffing and utilisation data shows that we have spare capacity somewhere in the firm to do exactly that role. Occasionally it requires a slight retooling of a senior associate's skills, but that's a much more certain investment than seeking an external candidate.*
>
> *When I push the requesting partner, he either thinks that a lateral hire will be quicker than retooling or wants to have the individual sitting in his own office for the convenience of communication.*
>
> *We have now implemented a more formal process for requesting a lateral. In the course of writing up the required business case, the partner often solves his own problem: by conferring with colleagues and gathering data about the request, he often uncovers the necessary expert already in-house. Now our requests are based strictly on specialised expertise that truly doesn't exist here or on strategic issues where the firm wants to grow – and the latter are typically instigated by members of the executive committee.*
>
> *So bottom-up requests have fallen enormously and we haven't suffered at all. Quite the opposite.*[28]

This point of view was echoed in similar conversations with a few leaders in other law firms, but too many firm leaders still fail to put the brakes on lateral hiring. To do so, you need both the willingness and the ability to enforce a more centralised approach in your firm. More on that point below.

Before your firm looks for an external hire for a business professional position, consider whether any of your existing lawyers want to transition to the business side of the firm. Today we see, for example, an increasing number of lawyers shifting into pure professional roles, such as chief client officer. Other examples include keeping the 'partner' title and status, but not performing billable work and instead dedicating the entire function to client relations. At international business law firm Osler, for example, one lawyer who practised for over 10 years is now titled 'Partner, Client Relations and Business Development Litigation', and dedicates over 95% of her time to client relations and development (see boxout for more details).

Case study: internal repositioning instead of external hire
Gillian is an experienced commercial litigator whose practice now focuses on client relations and business development rather than the delivery of legal advice.

She works closely with Osler's marketing and client relations team to promote the litigation department's dispute resolution and risk management services.

Externally, Gillian represents the department in a number of legal and industry forums, supports the pursuit of opportunities, and works to optimise the Osler experience by acting as a direct liaison with existing and potential clients as well as referral partners. Internally, Gillian supports her national litigation partners and associates in building their profile, identifying and pursuing new business opportunities and nurturing and growing firm-client relationships.

An easy way to open the door to admittedly sensitive conversations on internal transitions is to post an internal job listing and encourage internal applications. Providing transition opportunities to internal talent, and therefore drawing on existing resources, is an important step in the preparing to hire process for a number of reasons, including the following:

- **Less risk:** Trusted internal talent is much less risky than an unknown from outside the firm.
- **Retention of internal talent:** The firm might have an attorney who wants to make a move, to either another office or practice, but has not yet voiced that preference. For example, a new father may want to transfer from the demanding asset-based lending department to the more predictable trust and estates department, and possess the transferable skill set to do so. If he does not feel safe voicing his preference for the transition in the firm or simply is unaware of the opening because it was not

posted on an internal job board, then he may leave for a trusts and estates position at another firm.

- **Visibility of growth opportunities:** Posting jobs internally provides visibility to rising associates of where growth opportunities exist, and the transparency makes them feel more connected to overall management and firm strategy.
- **Hiring a unique contributor:** To make a lateral hire successful, you do not want to bring in an outsider who will 'compete' with someone already on your team who may have the same skill sets. Instead, you want to complement skills or add growth opportunities. Posting openings on an internal job board provides an opportunity for additional internal vetting – if the position directly competes with an existing attorney or professional, he or she can flag the overlap in skill sets and assist in modifying the job description appropriately. This process ensures that you are not only hiring to fill a technical gap, but are doing so in a way that sets the newcomer up for success in your firm culture and as a unique contributor on his or her particular team.

1.5 Create a data-driven business plan

Strategic considerations and financial models should answer the threshold question of whether the firm should hire. Factors such as expanding business opportunities, new offices in specific geographic markets, partner turnover and newly developed (or growing) practice or sector-focused groups should be considered. Analyse current capacity and utilisation to reveal whether the emerging market needs can be covered by an existing internal resource.

If a lateral is indeed the best option, then objectively gauge your firm's readiness to absorb the lateral. Has that office or practice just hired a cohort of other laterals who are consuming all the integration attention and energy? If a lateral partner is to be hired, is the practice group appropriately leveraged and will he or she have adequate associate support? Your ability to answer these questions ties directly to your ability to help a newly hired lateral succeed.

The analysis must not stop at high-level strategic considerations, however. **You need a robust, data-based analysis that forms the business case for each lateral hire. Many firms believe that they already have such a system in place, but most of the plans we have reviewed are more about arguments than analyses** – which is unsurprising, given that they were written by lawyers who had been neither supplied with data nor trained to perform quantitative analyses. Instead, engage your financial and business development experts to collect and dissect both internal and market data to calculate anticipated return on investment (ROI) for each proposed

"It's the leader's job to bring data – however imperfect and incomplete – to planning decisions. You need to look deeply at data from your clients and your firm to build insights and ultimately generate the best business case for investment."

Jennifer Scalzi, Calibrate Legal

candidate (see the Appendix for a template *pro forma*). Even more specifically as it relates to lateral lawyers, analysts should work with partners in both the proposing practice group and adjacent groups to understand a range of realistic scenarios and then calculate how sensitive the initial projected ROI is to these differing assumptions.

Case study: use of a central headcount committee

One firm with an advanced talent strategy has assembled a central headcount committee, comprising lawyers and human resources professionals, which governs lawyer hiring decisions globally. Practice groups create and submit a business case for hires. Then the committee meets monthly to decide which requests to approve or deny, based on the firm's strategy. This approach thus aligns the organisational and talent strategies. However, the process is quite lengthy and laborious and does not solve for accountability. The business plans submitted to the central committee set forth the argument for hire, but then are not revisited to see whether that argument held. Instead, accountability is left to the business performance of the practice area and, generally, whether the new lateral is performing. At best, the post-hire business case and performance is analysed on a general scale of 'bad, good enough or great', with little granular accountability.

If your firm decides that a lateral hire is the best option based on convincing evidence and a sound strategic plan, then you should produce a business plan towards that end. The plan should include firm or client-specific objectives, with a named individual responsible for seeing it through to completion. This plan should be developed for business professionals as well as attorneys. Accountability is critical.

1.6 Run analyses to track pockets of 'churn and burn'

Few firms get this right: you need hard data to uncover which practice groups and business functions have a track record for successful lateral hire integration. Firms are anecdotally aware of pockets of lateral lawyer 'churn and burn', whether that pocket is an office or a specific practice group. **Most firms have certain areas that continuously hire lateral lawyers and cycle through them quite rapidly. We have seen very few firms, however, that routinely or systematically collect that data and report on it, or use it as a basis for resource allocation going forward.** Firms have been performing analyses on why some lateral lawyer hires have succeeded and others have not, but these analyses tend to focus more on the individual lawyer – whether the lateral came as part of a group or had niche expertise – and not the organisational conditions that the lawyer joined. In other words, the analyses tend to point the finger at the lateral, but are not reflective in pointing the finger back at the firm and understanding the firm's role in creating conditions for success or failure across practice areas, offices, sectors, departments and so on.

Gather and review your lateral hiring data from the last five years or so, with a specific focus on who pushed for or sponsored the request, and how well each of those laterals fared once hired. An easy way to begin capturing this data is to track the number of hires retained in the past 100 days, 180 days, 12 months, two years – or whatever intervals make sense for your firm – as one of the key metrics to consider in lateral hiring. As shown in Table 4, the five-year attrition rates in Hugh Simons' 2017 research varied from 37% in litigation to a whopping 67% in bankruptcy practices.[29]

You may discover a strong correlation between certain partners' or practices' attempts and success rates or pockets of churn and burn. Do not be discouraged by a historically high churn rate. Instead, view it as a growth opportunity. Dig into it further by asking, "Why is that is so?" Generally, offending groups fail to strategically consider their hiring requests, use the wrong hiring criteria or lack the proper means to integrate laterals once they arrive. Gaining a full understanding of exactly what is broken helps a firm to pinpoint a sustainable, practical and long-term fix.

Table 4. Five-year attrition rate of lateral partners by practice area

Practice area	Five-year attrition
Litigation	37%
Alternative dispute resolution	39%
Antitrust	41%
IP litigation	43%
Real estate	43%
Taxation	45%
All practice average	47%
Corporate and securities	47%
Banking and financial institutions	53%
Intellectual property	55%
Energy	60%
Bankruptcy	67%

Source: Hugh A Simons, "Global Lateral Hiring by The Numbers: A Look Behind the High 5-Year Attrition Rate", The American Lawyer International, *3 February 2017*

1.7 Define the role and articulate the required capabilities

It is hard to measure the ROI on a new hire if you are not clear on what he or she was supposed to do in the first place. This phenomenon is true for partners, but is particularly pronounced for lateral business professionals and associates.

With respect to partners, the hiring partner should have a clear view on what role the lateral candidate will play based on the business plan supporting the decision to hire. The role could be to build business in a specific industry sector or contribute a needed kind of expertise to a particular client team. The firm should define the capabilities required to perform the role, including technical expertise, how well the person works on and contributes to teams, and leadership and management skills. What we see, however, is that even when firms set forth these sorts of aspirations in a business plan, they fail to define the capabilities required. Instead, they default to hiring the candidate who promises to port the largest book of business to the firm.

Point in practice: need to align evolving expectations

In my first legal marketing position, I was hired in a mid-sized US firm as the director of marketing and communications. In my interviews with the partners, they had told me that the objective for the position was to gain better visibility and better clients. I then walked in on my first day and one partner's legal secretary said, "Oh, good. I'm so glad that you're here. We have contact information for clients in four different databases, three of which are Excel spreadsheets with inconsistent column and row designations. Could you get started on consolidating these? The partners want to get a mailing out and it would be so much easier to do from one central database."

I was stunned and thought, "Am I reporting to the legal secretary or the two partners who just hired me for, as they put it, my strategic thinking?" We worked through things, and as I got on in years and the firm grew, there became the question of, "Well, if we have 20 practice groups and she's really helping three with their marketing plans, why isn't she helping the other 17?" But law firms habitually underinvest in professional staff and I didn't have the capacity to help all 20 practice groups. The firm didn't communicate this self-imposed bottleneck to my team's ability to allocate resources evenly across groups, which created unnecessary tensions between my group and the attorneys. There was always someone disappointed and it really didn't need to be that way.

Chief client officer, global law firm

When it comes to business professionals, firms often hire thinking that the new executive will solve every challenge; but those same firms have not built consensus internally as to what they want that person to do. Clearly, if a firm does not know what it is hiring somebody to do, it is impossible to define what capabilities are needed for the undefined role. This challenge often arises with the CMO position. A firm will often believe this role is needed; but what exactly is that need and has the firm explicitly articulated and agreed on it? Is it a need for someone who will lead a sales team, optimise operations or run communications? Defining the need is critical because it is impossible to determine what capabilities you need for an undefined role. Further, if you fail to define the need and hire a traditional marketing person, offering a high salary and promising a strategic role for what really turns out to be a grinding operations position, then you have a

"Very often, firms hire marketing people and think that they're going to kind of save the world – I mean, whether it's the CMO or someone even below a CMO. But they haven't built consensus internally as to what they want that person to do. They're missing that step."

Chief marketing officer, global law firm

problem. The new hire will uncover the bait-and-switch, however unintentional, and will lose trust and any loyalty to the firm. In this instance, not only does the need remain unfulfilled, but you have thrown money at the problem in an unproductive and time-consuming process while the competition is getting ahead.

Articulating the capabilities needed in a position can be quite challenging, even at the associate level. Technical capabilities are fairly straightforward, but ambiguity lurks when it comes to cultural differences and what lawyers are accustomed to or how they prefer working – in other words, what made them succeed at their prior firm. These 'success traits' can vary across region and practice – corporate lawyers may think differently from tax lawyers, who may think differently from litigators and real estate lawyers. As a result, everyone involved in the hiring decision – from the external recruiter and practice group head to the internal talent professionals – must understand the capabilities needed to ensure that a lateral associate hire can succeed in a specific group, however defined.

1.8 Develop the talent pool

As the market for legal services evolves – including increased client demands, the influence and impact of technology and the continued emergence of alternative service providers – law firms will increasingly need different kinds of talent to meet these changing needs. Some firms have already made strides in identifying and embracing new talent, such as international law firm Orrick's hiring of three IT architects as the beginning of what the firm has coined Orrick Labs. In a move intended to keep it ahead of the market, Orrick created this in-house team to focus on "creating leading-edge, innovative legal service solutions to enhance quality, security and efficiency".[30] Other firms have already begun to redeploy lawyer talent. At Littler Mendelson, one of the firm's best litigators was instrumental in developing Littler CaseSmart (LCS), an innovative and value-based platform that unbundled and redesigned the way legal matters are handled. Once LCS was up and running, the firm approached the litigator – again, one of the firm's best – and asked him to stop litigating and focus on LCS full time. He did.

This type of market movement makes the provocative work of Professor Richard Susskind, renowned legal futurist at the Oxford Internet Institute, seem prescient. Susskind warns that legal professionals have less than five years to reinvent themselves from being world-class legal advisers to world-class legal technologists: "No longer will firms aspire to building large teams of junior lawyers as the basis of their profitability. 'To survive', in the memorable words of [US economist and Harvard Business School Professor] Theodore Levitt (in his seminal article, 'Marketing Myopia'), lawyers 'will have to plot the obsolescence of what now produces their livelihood'."[31]

We anticipate that new roles such as those at Orrick and Littler Mendelson will continue to emerge as law firms implement the changes necessary to 'survive' in the rapidly changing market. However, firms will need the right talent for these roles and must build the pipeline of diverse talent now in anticipation of filling them.

Before creating a strategy to develop the pool of talent, firms should build consensus on the capabilities they believe they will need to become or remain successful in the long term. In other words, where is the firm placing its bets? As Susskind famously warns, "lawyers should plan either to compete with machines (look for legal jobs that are likely to favour human capabilities over artificial intelligence) or to build the machines (aim to be directly involved in the development and delivery of new legal technologies and systems)".[32] If your firm takes this as true, then it should be betting heavily on technology and developing a robust pool of tech-savvy talent.

Another quickly emerging role is that of legal operations, defined as a multi-disciplinary function that optimises legal services delivery to a business or government entity by focusing on the 12 core competencies illustrated in Figure 7.[33] Many law firms that compete in technology, consumer goods and manufacturing, financial services, energy/oil and gas/utility, biotech/pharma/life sciences, insurance and healthcare are already investing on this front, and are developing their pipelines through participation in industry events and educational resources such as the Corporate Legal Operations Consortium.

Once your firm has decided where it wants to place its bets, you need to develop a multi-pronged strategy to source and develop talent. Some avenues to consider include the following:

- **Incentivise:** Offer recruitment bonuses and/or encourage your professionals to regularly reach out to potential candidates working in other firms. Be mindful, however, of the potential for this avenue to lead to pay inequities and a less diverse workforce.[34] In a study of 53,000 US workers, white women were 12% less likely to receive a referral, men of colour were 26% less likely and women of colour were 35% less likely.[35] To address this disproportionate effect, consider incentives that pay more for candidates who are currently underrepresented in your employee population.[36] For example, US multinational corporation and technology giant Intel is paying twice as much for diverse referrals.[37] The legality of this approach will vary

Figure 7. The Corporate Legal Operations Consortium's 12 core competencies

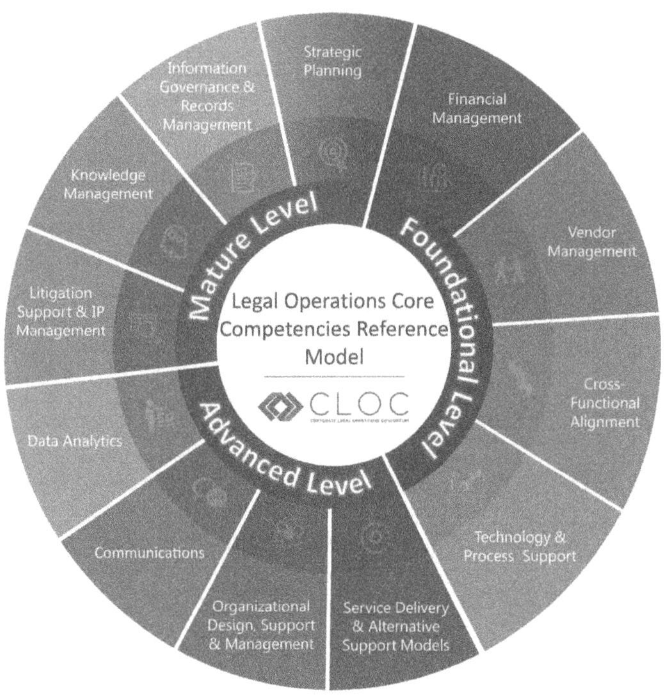

Source: © 2018 Corporate Legal Operations Consortium, Inc.

"What we've found is that typically, when we bring on a group of partners – let's say two to five or more who came from the same firm and already have a pretty established book of business and potentially have their own team – that has been more successful than not, and better than stars who we've gotten here and there that just take a lot longer to integrate."

Chief talent officer, AmLaw 50 firm

by jurisdiction. In the United States, however, the Equal Employment Opportunity Commission (EEOC) is the governing body and it prohibits employers from using neutral employment policies that have a disproportionately negative effect on applicants of a protected class.[38] Since employee referral programmes disproportionately benefit white men, Intel's programme to pay twice as much for diverse referrals is actually helping the company to comply with EEOC guidelines.

- **Leverage your networks:** Referrals from clients and industry contacts also provide leads to possible lateral hires, though the same diversity caveat applies.
- **Tap into alumni networks:** Keep a tight-knit alumni network. Ernst & Young reports filling around one-quarter of its vacancies in this manner.[39]
- **Hire an executive search firm:** Professional firms sometimes use search consultants for specialised lateral hires and rely on larger search consultants for international staffing needs, such as a new local office head (see below for tips on working with a search firm).
- **Train talent:** The talent that you need may not exist in the market, or it might be more effective to train talent to meet your needs. In either case, creating robust training programmes at your firm considerably opens up potential talent pools. Other

professional service firms have been doing this for some time. For example, while consulting firms traditionally targeted MBA students, they are becoming more willing to hire students with PhD degrees, lawyers and engineers and put them through business training. In 2010, McKinsey reported that only 44% of its consultants held an MBA, 24% a master's degree in another field and 22% an MD or PhD.[40]

- **Create and nurture the upstream pool:** A proactive talent strategy includes robust development of the upstream talent pool (ie, those coming up the ranks). Creativity here is key to outpacing the competition. Consider, for example, the following:
  - **Sourcing overlooked talent:** Tap into the myriad programmes that now exist to redeploy women returning from maternity leave. The OnRamp Fellowship, for example, is a re-entry platform that matches experienced lawyers returning to the workforce after a career hiatus with law firms and legal departments.[41]
  - **Starting early:** Consider implementing diversity programmes to offer internships to undergraduate and graduate business students. These students could prove the best candidates to fill some of the new roles that are emerging in today's legal services market.

1.9 Allocate the support necessary for success

Firm support is critical for lateral hires and you need to start lining it up in this stage, long before you begin the actual recruiting process. The type of support required will differ with each hire; firms should undergo a thorough review of the business plan for the newcomer in order to match the objectives with the support offered. An explicit conversation about resource allocation aligns expectations, ensures leaders' commitment and sets the stage for later holding people accountable for achieving a sufficient ROI. The types of resources required may be financial, cultural or internal, such as support staff, technology or even office location. For example, a partner who moves to a larger law firm with the goal of broadening his or her practice geographically should have robust travel support, including a designated budget, internal administrative help and introductions to key partners and clients in targeted locations. Further, the firm should consider whether lateral lawyers are being hired to explore new territory or exploit the firm's existing capacities.

Researcher Boris Groysberg distinguishes between star performers who are hired laterally to explore new sectors and those who are hired to exploit an existing service line, as well as those who are hired alone versus in a group.[42] For 'explorers', Groysberg has found that that solo stars suffer the biggest drop in performance, while those who move with colleagues suffer no significant decline in performance. This

Table 5. Relative success of acquiring lateral stars and groups to explore versus exploit

	Solo star	Team of lateral colleagues
Explore new sectors	Suffers biggest drop in both short and long-term performance.	No significant decline in performance.
Exploit existing service line	Suffers short-term drop in performance.	Best performance.

Source: Adapted from Boris Groysberg, Chasing Stars

finding intuitively makes sense. If a firm hires an attorney to explore a new sector, but does not have the existing resources in place to fully support his or her efforts, then performance will suffer. Alternatively, if the firm hires a team, then it is acquiring knowledge and capabilities that it currently lacks and team-specific performance dynamics that can support the star attorney(s) in the exploration. We note that the best-case scenario, however, is when firms hire teams of lateral colleagues to exploit an existing service line – presumably because of the existing institutional support. Generally, Groysberg's research indicates that the resources necessary for success in supporting lateral partners are already in place when their colleagues are hired as well.

For business professionals, the type of support required tends to be more complex. What support does a C-level business executive need in a law firm? First and foremost: respect. Historically, law firms have hired business professionals who have a background in law based on the argument that the professionals must understand what lawyers do – they must understand legal expertise – in order to perform their job successfully. The logic is sound. If we consider a corporate analogy, for example, a salesperson at a technology company must know the products to be competent and ultimately successful. What lawyers often fail to appreciate, however, is that this is a two-way street. Lawyers – who likely do not have the expertise of a chief financial officer or other executive – must work to understand the expertise that the business professional is bringing to the table. It is difficult to respect and value a professional when you cannot grasp or fully appreciate his or her contribution. And with an increase over the past eight years in law firms hiring business professionals from other professional service sectors – notably premier consulting, finance and sales organisations – firms will have to make an even more concerted effort on this front.

Two implications arise in this regard. First, although business professionals – unlike lawyers – do not have a licensing requirement to perform their work, their expertise is no less valuable to the firm. Second, although it is client-facing lawyers who typically get credit for generating revenue, their success in terms of both quality and volume often depends on support from business professionals.

Correcting these misconceptions is an important first step to adequately valuing business professionals and having the conversations necessary to determine and allocate the right resources – including reporting lines, financial allocations, support staff, internal networks and cultural support – upon hiring. We cannot emphasise the cultural component enough. All too often, firm partners fail to understand, and therefore recognise, the expertise and value that business professionals bring to the table, and this sentiment trickles down throughout the firm. Firm leadership must set the tone and embrace and foster the value of their business professionals; otherwise, they are setting them up for failure.

What can law firm leaders do to support mutual respect and appreciation of value among colleagues? De-categorisation and re-categorisation techniques can prove powerful in developing more meaningful intergroup contact among lawyers and business professionals. De-categorisation is aimed at the gradual dilution of intergroup barriers, while re-categorisation actively facilitates new and inclusive group dynamics. At the end of the day, the ideal interaction patterns are those that allow:

- equal status within the contact situation;
- the necessity for intergroup cooperation;
- common goals for the group; and
- formal and informal explicit support for the interactions.

As an example of de-categorisation and re-categorisation techniques in practice, consider a management consulting firm in the United Kingdom that established a cricket team which played one charity match a year with a London schoolboys' team. The team was composed of cricket enthusiasts from both the consulting pool and support staff. Even though the actual commitment – one Friday outing per year – was minimal, the nature of the interactions had far-reaching impacts among the 11 playing members who, over the course of time, increasingly stopped seeing each other through the prism of the class divide within the firm and built a genuine respect for each other centred around the love of a common sport. It led, among other things, to a 'cricket lovers mailing list' that remained active throughout the year and in which consultants and support staff both actively participated without inhibitions. Other research has shown that even relatively minor-sounding initiatives, such as wearing common sports jerseys, can reduce intergroup biases, as they force people to reconfigure their group alignments in subtle ways. Over a prolonged period and over multiple such interactions, the boundaries of class silos blur.

Point in practice: understanding and valuing the expertise of your colleagues
In the majority of law firms, tensions exist between the lawyers and the business professionals. To illustrate, consider a CMO. CMOs deal with two of the most sensitive matters of any partnership: client relationships and revenue. At the same time, CMOs cannot replace the revenue generation of lawyers and historically they were not given the resources needed to be truly effective in their roles.

For example, when business is good, a partner of a law firm will say, "Why do we need to pay almost $1 million to a CMO? We're shooting fish in a barrel. I can't keep up with the work." And yet, when business gets bad, they will say, "Why are we paying $1 million when, in fact, we see our revenue decreasing?" When the partners do not understand the value that business professionals offer, fail to provide the resources necessary for success – including cultural support and trust with sophisticated work – and compound these factors with unreasonable expectations, it is a lose-lose for all.

Instead, foster a culture of collaboration in which lawyers and business professionals can work side by side and truly understand the expertise and value of one another – from there, strong, trusting relationships will follow.

2. Stage 2: recruiting and interviewing

Although law firms today typically spend their greatest effort on the recruiting stage, our research has uncovered numerous ways to improve the process so that you reap the highest returns on that effort. The four steps we recommend in this section draw on both social science research and best practices from professional service firms to help guide you in optimising the recruiting and interviewing stage.

2.1 Search for capabilities over credentials

In Stage 1, you specified the capabilities that you wanted to recruit for by creating a job description tailored to your agreed needs and determining the capabilities required to succeed in the role. Now you need a process to ensure that you properly interview for these desired capabilities and not default to merely seeking credentials.

The risk of using the wrong criteria for hiring is especially acute when evaluating lateral associates or business professionals, and interviewers are also unnecessarily influenced by lateral candidates' CVs rather than their true capabilities. Law firms notoriously hire for credentials – what sociologist Lauren Rivera calls 'pedigree' – even though this approach is generally misguided.[43] While some credentials are proven predictors of success, others are false clues as to the candidate's future performance. For example, Professor Bill Henderson's research shows that:

> *Law school pedigree seldom, if ever, matters (and when it does, it could be negative). In contrast, grades are generally a positive predictor. Yet the relationship between grades and future performance may have less to do with cognitive ability and more to do with motivation. For example, we often find that membership on the law review is (after statistically controlling for grades) a negative predictor of future performance but publishing a law review note is a strong positive predictor. Why? Perhaps because the latter requires drive, persistence and/or intellectual curiosity, and presumably those are linked to on-the-job performance.*[44]

Point in practice: hiring for the capabilities needed to succeed at your firm

One firm hired a lateral associate to join its growing healthcare private equity group. The associate's CV listed a prestigious New England, United States boarding school where he was captain of the ski team, followed by an Ivy League college and law school, and included interests such as scuba diving and extensive travel. He had fantastic grades and was lateralling from a highly respected law firm. The associate lasted two years before he lateralled back to his old firm. In reviewing why this lateral hire had failed, the firm realised that while he had socioeconomic indicators that were similar to others who had succeeded at the firm, he had no 'hustle'. The associate had excelled in all of his pursuits, but his opportunities had been laid out for his choosing. Given this firm's eat-what-you-kill compensation model and the fact that the healthcare private equity group consisted of 'deal bros' who thrived on 'getting deals done', it is no wonder that this associate did not last. He had the technical expertise, but lacked the resourcefulness, resilience and drive necessary for on-the-job performance at this firm.

So why do law firms often default to relying on false clues? Often, when hiring business professionals, it starts with a failure to articulate the capabilities needed (as outlined in Stage 1, above). A prestigious firm hiring its first chief people officer might say that it wants

"A couple of years ago, a partner from an international firm called me asking for a COO referral. He said they really wanted to find someone from Accenture who had a graduate degree from MIT to help move their technology initiatives forward. I warned him that, while impressive, those credentials should not be the only thing they looked at in candidates: they should be a good fit for the job and other aspects of their background might be more informative. He responded, 'Trust me. We know what we're doing.' The person they hired was out the door a year later."

Former COO, AmLaw200 firm

someone from Bain Consulting who also has a Harvard MBA. However, these credentials do not necessarily equate to having the skills required to perform the job.

By way of analogy, consider the example of US department store JCPenney's former CEO, Ron Johnson. He was hired based on his track record at prestigious companies such as Apple (a multinational technology company) and Target (a US discount store retailer). But the knowledge and capabilities required in those positions did not translate to the position at JCPenney. He completely lacked awareness about the organisation's culture, brand and target consumer market. The company's sales dropped from $17 billion at his point of hire to $11 billion after only 17 months on the job.[45] Those who hired him had placed far too much value on his previous success at very different organisations and failed to consider whether his capabilities were relevant to JCPenney's situation.

Similarly, law firms are also prone to hiring individuals with certain firm or university names instead of homing in on capabilities, which can result in failed performance. Many firms seem fixed on this way of hiring, even when counselled by experts to consider other kinds of backgrounds. In our interview with an executive at a leading search firm, for example, he explained that he does not quibble with firm management about candidate credentials at the outset of a search: "If I start a search and I try to push down that barrier with the hiring committee, they're just going to throw up their hands and fight. The proof is when we start sending in candidates." Once the hiring committee spends time with candidates who the recruiter brings in because of their capabilities, and not just credentials, the committee 'gets it' and becomes open to different types of candidates. Without the benefit of such a strategic recruiter, however, firms may never even let those candidates in the door, never mind hire them.

Tips on working with retained executive search firms

- **Engage them earlier and co-create the job description:** Firms often deliver a job description to a recruiter with an instruction that the firm really needed the new hire 'yesterday'. In this way, they are missing the opportunity to sit down with their recruiters and have them help craft the job description based on the capabilities required for the job. It also puts unnecessary and possibly counterproductive strain on the relationship, as the recruiter is then put in the position of quickly finding candidates based on a job description that may or may not address the needs of the firm. This dynamic is especially poignant when hiring C-level executives, where the job descriptions are more nuanced.

- **Have patience:** You have entered into this agreement to make the right choice, not the fast one. Approach the joint venture as less of a transaction and more of a partnership. Executive search firms have vast connections and networks that span global markets. Sit down with them to have qualitative discussions, leveraging their expertise, to help your firm find the best possible selection for your needs.
- **Prevent bottlenecks:** Designate the COO or chief human resources officer as the point of contact, instead of the managing partner. The C-level officers can generally keep the process moving in a timelier fashion.
- **Be prepared for the interviews:** At the same time as you engage the search firm, create your interviewing plan – who in the firm is most qualified and appropriate to perform the interviews? The interviewers should be trained and prepared to assess for the relevant capabilities.
- **Keep up the momentum:** Once the process starts, timing is important. You must extend an offer before candidate interest wanes or superseding factors occur, such as a promotion or competing offer.

Source: www.forbes.com/sites/forbescoachescouncil/2017/05/17/tips-for-business-leaders-partnering-with-retained-executive-search-firms/#5066b7a46739

2.2 Evaluate candidates across four key capabilities

Hiring is greatly improved when organisations perform multiple interviews to triangulate on the following attributes:

- technical and leadership competence;
- collaborative capacity versus ability to develop, work with and leverage networks;
- cultural fit; and
- firm experience.[46]

We consider each in turn below.

(a) Technical competence

The technical competencies required for each position will vary based not only on the disciplinary expertise required for work product, but also on the managerial and leadership demands related to the role. For example, imagine that your firm is in the market for an M&A partner given heavy deal volume and a cohort of underperforming associates. You need to seek a candidate with not only the requisite M&A expertise, but also the management skills to help the department operate more efficiently and effectively. Ideally, this partner will also have a track record of leadership, having demonstrated a commitment to building a strong pipeline of qualified and motivated associates. If a team of associates is keen to follow the partner to your firm, that is a strong and credible indicator of leadership.

In considering business executives, now imagine you are a mid-sized firm in the market for a chief client growth officer with the overarching goal of the position to help the firm grow its client base to avoid acquisition. A candidate's business development expertise is critical, but maybe even more so is the ability to influence attorneys, engage a team, build momentum and energise the firm towards concrete objectives. Be careful of relying on false clues when assessing candidates for this type of technical competence and be sure to seek experience indicators that more accurately predict on-the-job performance.

One theme that kept emerging in our interviews was the challenge of creating a set of desired competencies when each practice group sought different traits in its lateral lawyers. As a result, the interview guidelines needed to be high level or else the partners in the practice group would dismiss the parameters as not relevant to their needs and discard them, going rogue and falling back on unstructured "Would I want to grab a beer with this person?" interviews.

"[Our interview guidelines were] very high level and the reason for that is because when you move into lateral [lawyer] hiring, the focus tends to be on technical ability and their experience. The variance between each practice area on what they were looking for, what they prioritised, meant that you had to bespoke it; and when you start bespeaking something, it means that the guidelines more or less need to be high level or they go out the window."

Former director of talent, magic circle firm

To hedge against this default tendency, you must invest in distilling the capacities required across practice areas. (Below we describe how to train interviewers on how to assess for these skills.) One firm took this charge very seriously and interviewed every practice group to determine how it defined success and what it perceived as the necessary competencies to succeed in that group. The firm then looked for commonalities and differences – not just across groups, but up and down seniority levels. It was tricky to find such commonalities, however, because people used different language to describe the same thing. As one executive at the firm recalled:

> *What we saw across all practice groups – no matter the age, gender, the practice, no matter who you're talking to – the whole concept of determination stood out. And people called it different things – someone who was 'all in', someone who would be open to 'just grinding'. That word was used lot.*
>
> *[This] certainly allows us to empower our lawyers to feel better equipped with respect to speaking to the types of skills that we're looking for, being able to fully engage and articulate them, and more importantly, being able to identify them when they see them. So that ultimately gets us to the point where we're making better matches and meeting the expectations of the people whom we're interviewing.*

(b) Collaborative capacity

Something required of all candidates – from partners to business executives and associates – in today's competitive environment is 'collaborative capacity'.[47] This refers to a candidate's suitability to become the kind of contributor who can truly leverage the firm's full set of expertise in order to solve both the firm's and its clients' most complex, high-value problems.

Once the candidate is in the chair, first use the kinds of behavioural questions described in section 2.3 to explore his or her past experiences with collaboration. Table 6 lists additional key competencies associated with strong collaborators, with sample prompts that the interviewer can use to probe.

Next, tackle collaboration head-on with the candidate. How can you directly assess a candidate's actual collaborative capabilities? Our advice is to get the issue on the table well in advance of the interview. **If you are using a search firm, make sure it is extremely well briefed on your demands for collaboration and is prepared to pre-screen candidates for this quality. Candidates turned off by this will rule themselves out.**

Table 6. Key collaborative competencies to test with candidates

Key collaborative competencies	Sample interview prompts to elicit example
• Adaptability • Conflict management • Initiative and follow-through • Integrity • Learning motivation/ curiosity • Listening and probing • Networking • Perseverance • Persuasiveness (leading without authority) • Political sensitivity	• Tell me about a situation when you teamed up with colleagues to solve a really tough client problem. • Follow-on: How did you find the right experts? How did you know they were capable? How did you convince them to join the effort? What role did you play after the team was formed? • Describe a time when you needed a colleague's input on client work, but that person did not respond to requests. What did you do? • Give me an example of a time when you uncovered an opportunity to serve a client with a multi-practice team. What ultimately happened? What role did you play in helping to build a committed and accountable team? How did the client respond? • How do you handle a situation when a colleague underperforms or does not meet expectations?

Source: Dr Heidi K Gardner

It is worth emphasising that collaborative capacity is an equally important trait among business professionals. In today's environment, COOs of law firms also need to be leaders in human resources, business development and other C-level functions. These executives need to have a deep appreciation and understanding of everyone who is sitting at the proverbial table, as these central functions now collaborate with each other to drive revenue opportunities. While this was unheard of pre-recession, that is no longer the case. The C-level mandate is no longer just about support; it is about actually driving a delivery system to clients.

(c) Cultural role and fit, and the diversity caveat

Turnover as a result of poor culture fit can cost an organisation between 50% and 60% of the person's annual salary.[48] Professional service firms, and especially law firms (see Figure 8), understand the importance of cultural fit and interview heavily for it.

Evaluators implicitly gravitate towards and explicitly fight for candidates with whom they feel an emotional spark of commonality. Professor Lauren Rivera's research of elite professional service firms shows that cultural reproduction in elite professional service firms

"One law firm hiring manager boasted: 'We have a weekend getaway for our new summer associates their first week here. When one of our summers got back the next week, he said to me, 'We're all so different in our different ways but you can tell we were all recruited because we all have the same personalities. It's clear like we're all the same kind of people.' "

Lauren Rivera, *Hiring As Cultural Matching*

Figure 8. Evaluators who ranked fit as most important criterion in job interviews, by firm type

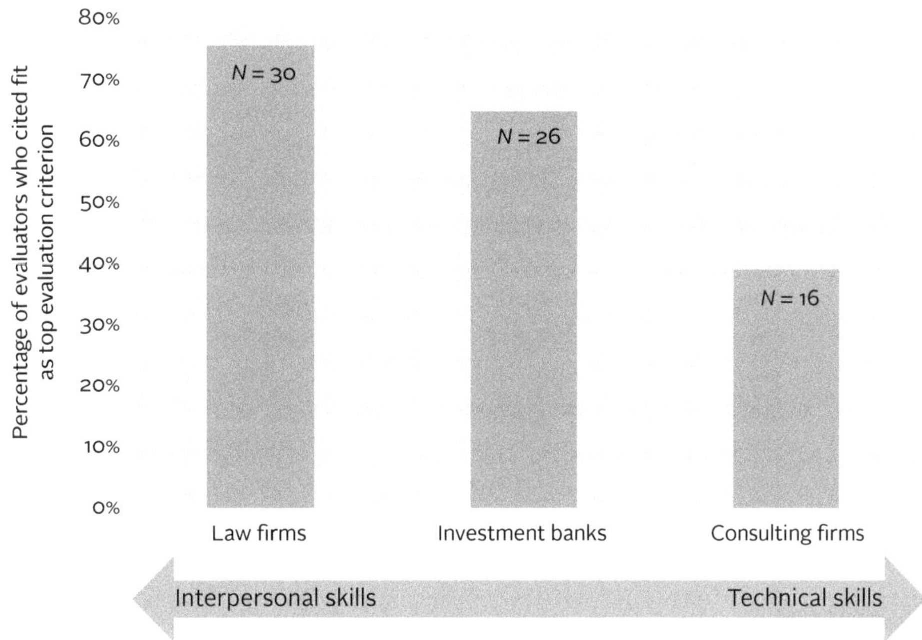

Source: Lauren Rivera, Pedigree: How Elite Students Get Elite Jobs

produces new hire classes that mirror "firms' existing employees in cultural signals and lifestyle markers".[49] Cultural cohesion is the glue that can hold firms together through good times and bad; but an obvious implication of placing significant weight on similarities is the potential for hiring a demographically homogenous workforce. In Rivera's research, interviewers favoured extracurricular activities associated with the white upper-middle class that were acquired through intense, prolonged investment of material resources and time not only by job applicants, but also by their parents.[50] Further, she found that: "Given that less affluent students are more likely than upper-middle-class students to believe that achievement in the classroom rather than on the field or in the concert hall matters most for future success and focus their energies accordingly the types of cultural similarities valued in elite firms' hiring processes had the potential to create inequalities in access to elite jobs based on parental socioeconomic status."[51]

Even firms which espoused a commitment to diversity still used a process that had a disproportionately negative effect on socioeconomically diverse candidates. Firms that devoted significant resources to increasing diversity still held the belief that achieving a baseline of cultural similarity represented recruitment success.[52] In essence, these firms sought surface-level diversity, but still prized deep-level (ie, cultural) homogeneity in new hires.[53] This is not the type of diversity that produces the variety of ideas, perspectives and attitudes that lead to superior team performance; it only serves to produce a population of people who may not look the same.

In addition to assessing for cultural fit, firms must have candid conversations about the role responsibilities – both good and bad. Every job has its challenges. Think of interview conversations and the process leading up to hire as creating what organisational behaviour expert Denise Rousseau has coined the 'psychological contract'.[54] This contract governs expectations in the reciprocal obligation between the firm and the new hire. By having honest conversations with candidates about the position's opportunities and potential difficulties, the firm develops an authentic relationship that will inspire loyalty once the candidate joins the firm, and avoids the risk of new hires feeling that they have experienced a 'bait and switch'. Firms that provide a realistic job preview also help candidates to opt out if they realise that it is not a good role fit. It is cheaper and more reliable for candidates to opt out of the process early than to proceed when they are ultimately a bad fit for the job, and this self-selection will result in a hire who is ultimately a superior fit.

(d) Firm experience

Hire lateral partners from firms that are less profitable: An important factor to consider in lateral partner hiring is the profitability of your firm compared to the profitability of the lateral partner's former firm.[55] It matters whether the lateral partner moves to a firm that is higher or lower than his or her prior firm in profits per partner rankings. In general, lateral partner hires who move to higher-profit firms are more successful than those who move to lower-profit firms, likely because they are given a larger platform and more resources to fuel practice growth. This finding suggests that hiring partners should 'hire from below', or be thoughtful and strategic about the value proposition and business plan that the firm is offering the incoming partner.

Consider caveats in hiring lateral business professionals without law firm experience: Generally, law firms have shown increased interest in hiring business professionals from outside of law to introduce thought leadership from other professions and keep ahead of the competition. Infusing diversity of thought and best practices from other professions into a law firm is a great strategy, when done correctly. Two caveats to consider here are:

- demonstrated ability to operate in a conservative environment; and
- ability to understand the 'law firm client' and tailor best practices to fit the firm.

Figure 9. Less profitable firms face a disadvantage in lateral partner hiring: Among the AmLaw 100 firms, those with the lowest profitability had five-year attrition rates of lateral partners, which were nearly double the rates of their most profitable peers – despite roughly similar levels of overall hiring. Benchmarking your firm relative to true peers in this regard allows you to anticipate more realistically the likelihood of lateral hires' success.

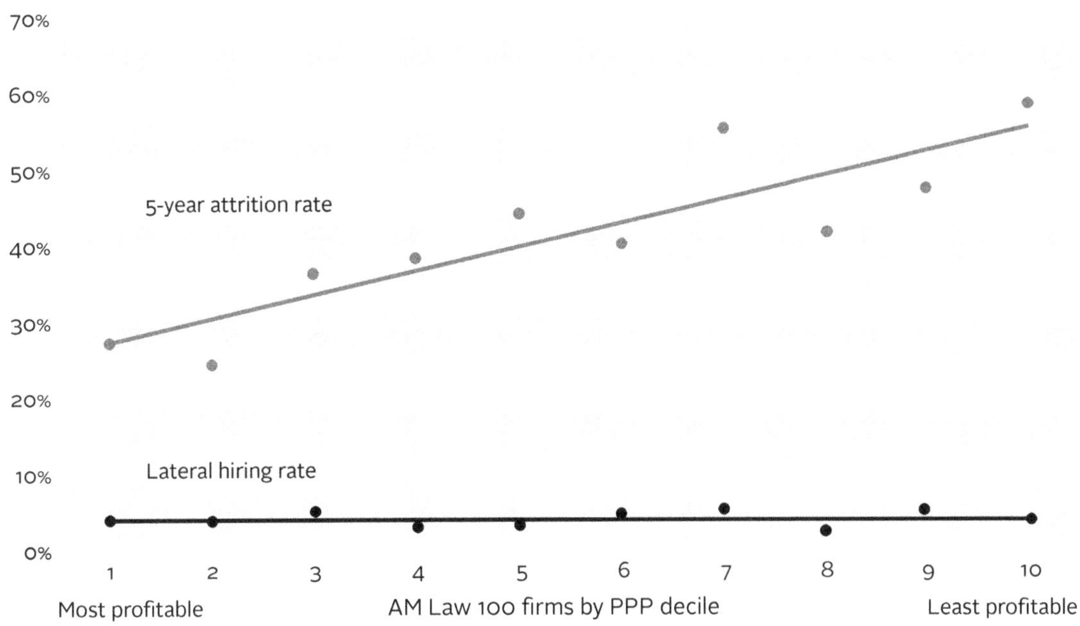

Source: Hugh A Simons, "Global Lateral Hiring by The Numbers: A Look Behind the High 5-Year Attrition Rate", The American Lawyer International, *3 February 2017*

Law firms are a lagging, not a leading, indicator of change.[56] Thus, in addition to the requisite transferable skills, the incoming executive must have the patience, resilience, tact and stamina to move initiatives forward in the slow-moving law firm environment. Further, if, for example, the firm hires an executive from McKinsey to bring and implement best management practices, the firm must manage expectations around this objective – how quickly is he or she expected to implement changes and will he or she have the resources and support to do so?

This leads to the second caveat: a business professional needs the ability to learn law firms and how best practices from other professions must be adapted and customised to fit the unique needs of a law firm. If it were as easy as picking up a best practice from McKinsey and layering it over the law firm, then this would have been done by now. It is more complicated than a mere overlay and incoming executives need not only to understand this, but to embrace it as part of their charge.

2.3 Identify and train people to conduct behavioural-based interviews

Assuming that your firm has a job description that fills the skills gap felt at the firm and incorporates the capabilities necessary for success, and that you are getting the right candidates in the door for interviews, the third piece of critical importance is training the interviewers to interview for capabilities.

Some law firms already have well-established processes for assessing a candidate's merits – especially a lawyer's technical capabilities and often his or her reputation with clients. These firms put interviewees through dozens of unstructured interviews with staff members and partners, in multiple geographies and offices. If those processes are actually getting the results you want, then use them. But consider augmenting them with best practices from other professional service firms outside of law, where interviews are structured to assess for specific competencies.

Structured interviews that elicit specific capabilities that match the job responsibilities result in superior performance. A review of the research literature gives us reason to expect that they could improve the correlation between interviews and work performance from .38 to .52.[57] Structured interviews are also better for overcoming implicit bias. As Iris Bohnet, Roy E Larsen professor of public policy and behavioural economist at Harvard Kennedy School, advises: "[Unstructured] interviews should not be your evaluation tool of choice; they are fraught with bias and irrelevant information. Instead, managers should invest in tools that have been shown to predict future performance. On the top of your list should be work-sample tests related to the tasks the job candidate will have to perform. For example, Compose, a cloud storage company, decided to completely do away with résumés and instead evaluate job candidates based on how well they solved a job-related problem."[58]

In the law firm context, very few firms have equipped their partners and other interviewers with the training and tools necessary to assess somebody through an interview for particular competencies – a more precise process than walking away with only vague impressions of the 'cultural fit'. In other professional service firms, such as McKinsey, interviewers are trained to zero in on one specific capability and are given the tools to do so. The interviewers have clear types of questions, including case studies, and a whole rash of different techniques, both structured and unstructured. To achieve this level of sophistication and data-driven hiring, the firm first must define the capabilities necessary for the role and then interview for them. The interview process should be structured into:

- behavioural interviews targeted at specific capabilities;
- qualification scores on specific metrics; and
- interview debriefs.

The best practice in creating structured interviews is to use behavioural questions, rather than hypothetical questions. Behavioural questions elicit insight into candidates' problem-solving approaches and emotional intelligence – skills important for partners, business professionals and associates alike. The theory is that the best predictor of future behaviour is past behaviour in similar circumstances that either were recent or reflected long-standing behaviour patterns. Candidates are asked to describe particular situations they have faced, how they handled them, their personal emotional response and perhaps what they learned from the experience. The objective is to break the candidate out of predictable and standard responses and enable the interviewer to gain a situational context for the candidate's emotional response.

Each behavioural interview question should have a learning objective behind it. The question should be crafted to assess a technical, collaborative or cultural capacity or behaviour, and whomever creates the question should produce a 'best practice' answer to the question with delineated criteria. Interviewers can then structure the interviews by organising these questions into an agenda, walking through the questions with the candidate and simultaneously scoring the candidate's answers against the 'best practice' criteria. In addition to the numerical scores, firms should encourage interviewers to submit a qualitative, holistic assessment of the candidate that can be considered along with the metrics.[59]

Point in practice: behavioural questions
Can you provide me with an example of when you made a bad decision?

Follow-on questions might include the following:

- How did you feel?
- Did you take steps to rectify it?
- Did you take the hit or try to minimise the fallout?

Empower your lawyers to follow their curiosity, instead of treating the interview like a deposition or cross-examination. Keep digging based upon the candidate's emotional response to each question and examine the candidate's thought process.

2.4 Determine key qualifications and assign scores to each
In addition to scoring the candidate on behavioural criteria in the interview, identify the key qualifications or prior experience that sets someone up for success for the role. Ask interviewers to assign scores to each of the qualifications and include them in the hiring decision. There is room to get creative – for example, you could ask interviewers to score the candidate's CV or references.[60]

You could also engage the candidates in this fact-finding expedition. For example, consider Figure 10, which lists a number of values on the horizontal axis and a score of 0 to 6 on the vertical axis. At a 100-year old white shoe law firm with few lateral hires, the values of the firm would likely centre around collegiality, teamwork, informal structures and prestige. In asking a candidate who has performed well and thrived for many years at an 'eat-what-you-kill' law firm to rank his or her values on the same scale, you can spot potential cultural fit challenges that may require further discussion with the candidate.

Obviously, this kind of interviewing is new for many partners. It requires training and practice, which many will resist. But consider this: many of the same probing, listening, analysing and empathy skills that are essential for interviewing are the same skills that astute advisers

Figure 10. Value alignment diagnosis

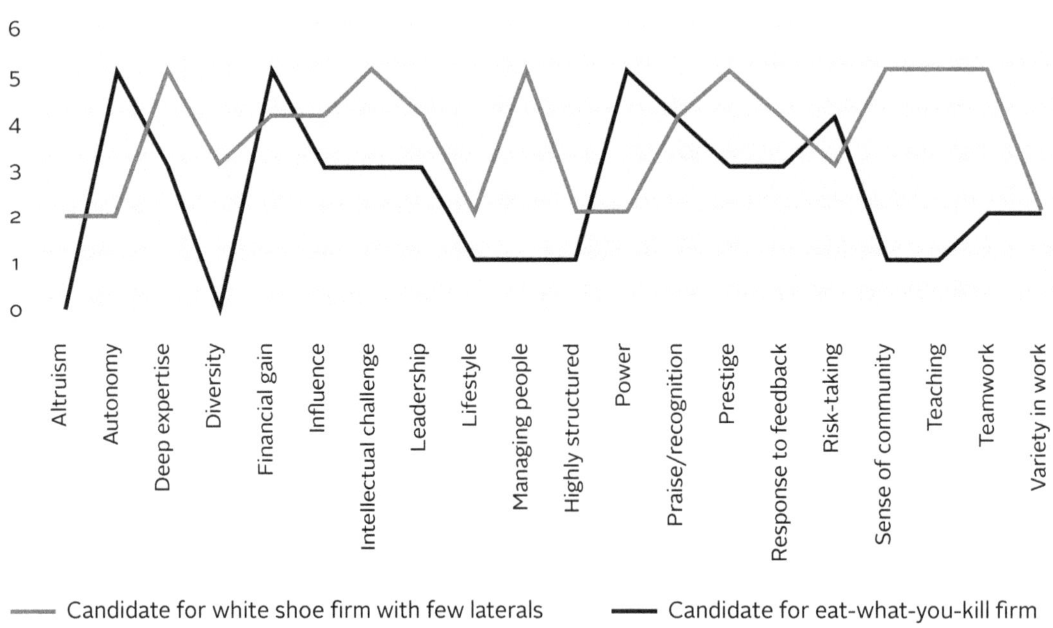

Source: Dr Heidi K Gardner and Anusia E Gillespie

"Improving the quality of assessments is 3x more profitable than increasing the size of the candidate pool, and 6x more profitable than getting the chosen candidate to accept a lower compensation package."

Boris Groysberg. "The Definitive Guide to Recruiting in Good Times and Bad", *Harvard Business Review*, May 2009

use with clients to uncover and understand complex business issues. So the partners who become excellent spotters of collaborative candidates are those who are better equipped to discover client opportunities where those candidates' expertise could be useful. You can use this point as a way to convince reticent or self-interested partners to participate in the training. And consider that excellent professional service firms that take interviewing seriously make training mandatory for all interviewers, even those who 'only' do campus recruiting.

2.5 Use the interview data to debrief and make decisions

All too often, law firms still hold lengthy meetings where they discuss the merits of all the candidates and argue about who gets the offer. This is not only time consuming, but it can also introduce arbitrary influences – such as overweighting the opinions of those who speak loudest – into the hiring process. Further, these meetings are often held days or weeks (or, let's face it, months) after the actual interview took place. This time lag could skew impressions and result in an overweighting of the most recent interviews, since they are freshest in people's minds.

Firms should consider doing away with this antiquated process. Interviewers at renowned consulting firms such as Bain and McKinsey submit their data through standardised reports almost immediately after an interview.[61] Law firms should strive for this standard – quantify your qualitative information as much as you can and have your interviewers submit the information the same day as the interviews. Tally the data and use this information as the primary input for hiring; any deviation should be examined for bias or other untoward influences.[62]

2.6 Close the deal

At least one of your five best candidates is likely to turn down your offer.[63] It is critical after interviewing to maintain contact with candidates and express the firm's sincere interest in and support of their goals. If working with a recruiter, allow the recruiter to extend the offer and discuss terms – this is his or her expertise, after all. Otherwise, senior partners should typically call candidates with offers and share with them their passion for the firm and answer any last questions.

Often, it can be helpful to have the same person who made the offer to the individuals (usually a senior partner) follow up with candidates as they make their decisions. However, this should not occur to the exclusion of associates. They are often great at selling the business and can also support a final quality check on candidate fit. It is likely that some partners and associates will be stronger than others at providing this support; identify the closers within your own firm to make the process more effective.

Successful professional service firms make sure that in closing the deal, they remain true to the values and style they have tried to project during the rest of the process. A firm's approach to finalising hiring needs to be consistent with its values and give candidates a chance to step back should they spot a disconnect between their values or goals and those of the firm.

3. Stage 3: integration

Firms that analyse their own cultures, pinpoint desirable attributes of existing players and hire for those attributes will best assimilate and retain talent. That edge is a true competitive advantage in today's hot labour market. In addition to the lateral hire's ability to 'hit the ground running' and higher likelihood of staying with the firm with proper integration, successful integration colours the lateral's perception and therefore experience of the firm and can influence team performance.

3.1 Make laterals' experience meaningful from Day 1 and start even before they officially join

Lateral hires judge their new position, new colleagues and new environment the minute interviews begin and then with earnest in the first week of hire. These interactions and associated judgements produce a halo effect, with lasting implications. The biggest innovation in induction integration is the length of time allocated. In other professions, it goes on for six months. Induction happens before Day 1 and and continues for half a year, with continual check-ins and training involved throughout that time, rather than being front-loaded.

Cutting-edge companies appreciate that of all the important new hire experiences, an employee's first day on the job is especially powerful and symbolic. The best organisations use various processes and tools to pave the way (eg, see Table 7). Leading technology companies take it to the extreme and have processes laser-focused on the first 45 minutes of a new hire's first day. If a new hire is not productive in the first 45 minutes of employment, then Facebook considers that a failed onboarding process.

Table 7. Integration highlights at leading technology companies

Company	Process
Facebook	**The 45-minute rule** Facebook employees are productive within 45 minutes of walking through the door on their first day. Anything less is considered a failure on the part of the department. Facebook achieves this by calibrating all systems and devices (eg, PCs, phones) before the new hire's first day. It also places a keen focus on discussing the practical aspects of the job, such as how to set up a meeting or use the printer.
Google	**Just-in-time reminder checklist** A reminder email is sent to the new employee's manager the day before the employee's first day. The checklist prompts managers to complete five small tasks proven to have the highest impact on the productivity of the new hire: • Have a discussion about roles and responsibilities. • Matching the new hire with a peer buddy. • Help the new to hire build a social network. • Set up employee onboarding check-ins once a month for the new hire's first six months. • Encourage open dialogue. This process has improved employee onboarding results by 25%.

Sources: https://blog.capabiliti.co/employee-onboarding-facebook-google-apple/; www.inc.com/laura-montini/facebook-cio-45-minute-onboarding-rule.html; www.tinypulse.com/blog/companies-with-the-most-unique-employee-onboarding-practices

"We certainly found that using the art gallery technique meant that people could spend longer or less time on the areas they were interested in and they absorbed the activity more than having someone talk through lots of pictures on a PowerPoint slide."

Director of talent, leading accounting firm

Although Day 1 induction in law still tends to be a day spent with HR and PowerPoint, more advanced industries are including this dry, technical integration in the pre-induction training. For these industries, Day 1 induction is about rolling out the red carpet and managing first impressions. The experience is used to make the lateral feel that he or she is really wanted at the firm, and that incumbent employees and executives are excited to have him or her join. While this experience used to vary by geography, there is a move towards a global induction experience to ensure that induction is consistent no matter where you join and to which practice area or department.

What does this Day 1 experience look like? Of course, it depends. You can allocate more resources and time with a group of lateral partner hires than with a single CMO integration, for example. For group integration, specialised consulting firms exist to create blended learning techniques, deliver technical training while leveraging firm expertise by incorporating partner stories and gamifying the learning process. For example, one major accounting firm created an art gallery where different people in the firm had done pro bono work or contributed to charity projects, and the laterals were led by a tour guide through the art gallery and learned how they could use their expertise in a pro bono way globally. Whatever creative process you choose, the point is to consider the dual objectives of making the lateral hire feel welcomed and wanted, and getting him or her up to speed on both technical and cultural training. This is a place where, if you are deliberate and thoughtful, you can create a customised win-win.

The most innovative, talent-driven firms understand how best to use the time immediately before a new hire officially joins the firm. For many, this pre-joining induction consists predominantly of an online integration system. In the past, this focused more on the procedural documents that the lateral needed to have signed and the details of his or her qualifications; but increasingly there is a cultural element to these online portals. Companies are introducing video elements welcoming people to the firm, and many features that are generally considered best practice in entry-level hiring are now moving into lateral hiring. Organisations also provide senior people with access to their email and text systems long before Day 1 of employment because the email content and culture provide such rich information to the lateral. In this way, the lateral learns about current transactions, the players at the firm and the different styles of communication. Firms may throw their hands up at confidentiality and conflict issues, but we are confident that you can find a way to implement this practice.

Inside the firm, too, it takes significant preparation to ensure that the new hire has a meaningful first day on the job. At Google, the new employee's manager receives an emailed checklist the day before a new hire joins his or her team, completion of which has improved employee onboarding results by 25%.[64]

Many law firms have their own version of an integration checklist, which includes items down to the details of introducing the new hire to departmental colleagues. As we discuss below, however, accountability is often lacking in law firms, and managers who are not held accountable often skip items on the checklist or otherwise delegate them to someone more junior.

Lateral associates essentially receive an 'integration-light' version of onboarding. One professional from a leading law firm observed that the success of integration was quickly seen in team performance: poor integration created "high-drama" teams with constant in-fighting and reporting to human resources. On the flipside, strong integration created "low-drama" teams with positive cultures and stellar performance. As he explained, when you follow best practices for lateral integration: "You're going to create and foster the environment that you want within your team. Less drama; people pay attention to performance and do what they need to get things done. And there will be lower turnover rates and there will be less people calling out at the last minute because they are ill and need vacation. It just happens."

“[The checklist] included a whole list of items that they made sure every new hire went through in the firm, and they really held the managers accountable for making sure that things happened that were on that – including, if it was on the list, making sure that the manager introduced the new hire to everybody in the department. It was shocking to see how many times, if that wasn’t on the list and they weren’t held accountable for it, a manager would not even take the time to introduce a new hire to the other people in the department or assign it to somebody else senior, who could introduce those people to the department.”

Former partner, large international law firm

Surprisingly, for business executives, we were unable to find any deliberate practice of integration. For business professionals, we heard that firms do their best to ensure that the person can participate in training programmes and is encouraged and perhaps supported in meeting colleagues; but that's it. We encountered pushback on the lack of professional integration, the thrust of which was that business professionals are more resourceful than lawyers and therefore know how to integrate themselves in the firm. Others conceded that the firm should probably spend more time on this. Clearly, law firms need integration processes for business professionals and should prioritise building them based on the best practices outlined above for other lateral hires.

Continuing integration predominantly consists of post-hiring mentoring and accountability, as described below. However, building in a culture of consistently engaging and welcoming the lateral over the first six months of employment is also critical. Otherwise, the firm risks the lateral feeling as though the Day 1 induction was disingenuous and, worse, that the policy and procedures at the firm are inconsistent with the true culture it embraces.

3.2 Acquaint with the culture and shape processes around new hires' strengths

Integrating new lateral hires requires tailored, often individualised, approaches to helping them adjust to the culture. Strong integration programmes address potential challenges upfront and understand that full integration is a long-term process that requires structure, feedback and commitment from both the firm and the new recruit. That said, there are finite resources for new hire integration and firms face financial trade-offs when designing these programmes. Off-site multi-week training and initiation rituals are rarely the right answer for law firms, even though they are commonplace among the best consulting firms, for example. In all cases, firms must ensure that there are appropriate resources focused on integration processes and produce a programme that at least includes education about the following:

- the firm's vision statement, general direction and strategic plans – and, most importantly, how the newcomer fits into these plans;
- the management and structure of the firm and the office, and key information about staff;
- an overview of the factors affecting firm profitability, how the firm calculates utilisation and realisation rates and, for lawyers, policies and procedures related to non-billable time, inputting time and billing and collections;
- HR information and basic work processes; and
- details on how the lateral hire is expected to assimilate.

Lateral hires bring their own set of integration challenges. Senior professionals will have developed a strong cultural fit with their prior firm and may find it difficult to adjust to a new firm's cultures. Another issue is that professionals in the hiring firm may defend their turf against what they see as the threat of encroachment by a newly hired senior colleague.[65] Some leading firms, such as Wachtell, Lipton, Rosen & Katz, have therefore prohibited lateral hiring in an effort to preserve their unique culture.[66] In firms that continue to hire laterals, the best address potential turf issues head-on and find ways to initiate collaboration among colleagues.

Another lateral integration challenge revolves around the lateral's sense of self and the expectations related to his or her assimilation into the firm's culture. **Instead of a sole focus on the firm's culture, consider shaping entry processes around how the individual is expected to offer his or her unique contributions to strengthen the firm.** This individual-identity conditioning and the resulting authentic self-expression have beneficial effects on employees' attitudes at work, such as their engagement and job satisfaction, as well as reducing turnover and enhancing performance.[67] Making authenticity an explicit value from the start of employment not only inspires greater commitment and effort, but can also produce the type of 'positive deviance' that will afford your firm the agility and fresh thinking necessary to get or stay ahead in the competitive market for legal services.[68]

Immersive cultural integration at Zappos
Five-week training and financial offer to leave the company

Zappos, an e-commerce footwear company owned by Amazon, offers employees a five-week course that teaches them everything they need to know about company culture and values. At the end of the course, employees are offered $2,000 to leave if they don't think they're the right fit.

Only about 1% of new hires have historically taken the $2,000 financial incentive to leave the company.

Source: www.tinypulse.com/blog/companies-with-the-most-unique-employee-onboarding-practices

3.3 Assign a peer mentor

Most firms already have a nominal 'buddy system' for incoming hires, but far too few of those programmes actually work. These programmes typically fail due to a lack of trust and established relationship between the mentor and mentee. A simple designation as mentor/mentee on paper does not establish a relationship in reality; **firms need to take**

proactive measures to ensure that the mentor proactively engages and make himself or herself available to the mentee, and that the mentee trusts the mentor so that he or she feels safe in asking the questions necessary to successfully navigate office dynamics.

To create the highest chances of a lateral hire being successfully integrated, you need to take some specific steps to ensure that mentoring happens (in multiple directions, as discussed below), and that all parties are held accountable for delivering post-hire collaboration within the first 12 months.

For lateral partners and business professionals, these steps include the following:

- Assign peer mentors for new hires to help them learn the firm's culture – insiders, such as people who serve as 'honest brokers' in the firm to help connect partners with client or other work. Ideally, these mentors will be people whom the new hires met and connected with during the recruiting process, so that they have already established a level of interpersonal trust.
- Gain commitment from a few specific people in the hiring group (practice, office or ideally both) who are responsible for introducing newcomers to several pre-determined accounts or other kinds of strategic contacts, as outlined in the pre-hire business plan. And require them to report on progress – to firm leaders, or at least their practice leader (whose feet you then hold to the fire), not to a functionary in HR. Again, the key here is specificity and accountability.
- Hold formal internal roadshows for laterals to present their client work to offices, practice groups and sectors. Make sure the local leader has spoken with the lateral ahead of time to suggest specific people or account opportunities that the lateral can reference during the presentation, and to ensure that the highest-potential collaborators attend the roadshow.

Steps specific to lateral partners, and to some extent associates, include the following:

- Work with laterals as soon as they join to develop a strategic client service plan, which identifies specific opportunities for them to involve incumbent partners. Leaders should facilitate those introductions and make it clear to incumbents that they are expected to participate.
- Use competency grids to assess the collaborative and mentoring abilities of both the newly hired partner and those in the surrounding practice. (If you do not have these tools, your professional development staff need to source or create them.)

3.4 Assist new joiners in building their networks

When it comes to retention, bigger networks are not better networks and, in fact, are often related to turnover because eager newcomers waste time on developing unproductive connections. The implication for law firms is that the current best practice of sending new partners, for example, on a 'world tour' where the partner visits many or even all of the firm's offices – no matter how far-flung – may not be the best practice. The world tour is meant to embed new partners in the fabric of the firm; but if the partners do not come away with established interpersonal trust and relationships, a strong knowledge of colleagues' expertise and significant brand exposure and visibility for their own practices, then this approach will not result in successful integration and retention. Instead, firms should follow the guidelines, above, for making a roadshow productive.

The research of Professor Rob Cross shows that the qualities of an individual's network that are associated with low turnover in an employee's first year are different from the qualities that ensure retention in Years 2 to 5.[69] In their first year, new hires need networks that jumpstart productivity and inclusion; while in Years 2 to 5, employees need networks that drive collaborative efficiency and generate a sense of purpose in their work.[70] The activities associated with this network transformation are summarised in Table 8.

The key insight is that the most successful and committed long-term employees are those who transform their networks from an initial focus on productivity and inclusion to a focus on efficiency and purpose. Leaders play a critical role in facilitating this network generation and transformation, and it all starts through a strategic emphasis on the lateral integration process. Accordingly, instead of a rapid-fire approach to socialising new hires, consider a deliberate social capital strategy that evolves with the needs of the lateral hire.

3.5 Hold new joiners, the hiring partner and peers accountable for success

As discussed in Stage 1, creating an agreed-upon business plan with projected ROIs is critical because without a concrete plan, it is impossible to hold anyone accountable for results (see section 1.5). Law firms are notoriously bad at holding their lawyers and professionals directly accountable. Instead, firms tend to rely on a vague notion of reputational accountability – that is, people will perform to maintain their reputations, even if no one is monitoring them.

For example, a practice leader who advocates for and successfully brings a new partner on board is typically not directly accountable for that new partner's performance. Aside from reputation for making a

Table 8. Social capital needs in Year 1 and Years 2 to 5 of employee tenure

Employee social capital needs over time	
Year 1	**Years 2 to 5**
Become valued resources that are sought out and 'pulled' into the organisation (rather than 'pushed' in by the new hires proclaiming intelligence or touting their experience from a past working life). **Example:** Assign a third party – either a mentor, marketing professional or other – to serve as the new hire's ambassador and spread knowledge of his or her expertise through word of mouth or other communications.	Craft collaboratively efficient interactions that reduce overload, and create time and space for people to build enterprise-wide networks. **Example:** In performance reviews have conversations around efficiencies and empower the hire – through cultural, financial and other resource support – to create a system or process that will make his or her work easier to perform.
Engage with similarly tenured employees for acculturation and a sense of belonging. **Example:** Place the new hire on a committee.	Engage in collaborations that yield a sense of purpose in one's work. **Example:** Suggest and allocate pro bono activity if the lawyer demonstrates interest.
Connect with key opinion leaders in networks for information to help do their job and, just as importantly, benefit from the reputation and legitimacy that accrue through these ties. **Example:** Create customised tour for the new hire to meet key people at the firm and work with the new hire to provide continued value to those people – for example, by providing market intelligence on a client or otherwise demonstrating a 'giver mentality'.	Build non-insular networks rich with boundary-spanning ties that make employees more innovative and effective in the organisation. **Example:** Involve the lawyer in a cross-disciplinary focus group to analyse a business challenge and provide advice to management.

Source: R Cross, et al, Connect and adapt *(Organ Dyn, 2017), http://dx.doi.org/10.1016/j.orgdyn.2017.08.003*

good hire, the only way the practice leader is held accountable is indirectly through compensation. The rationale is that if the lateral partner performs poorly and the practice area suffers as a result, the practice leader's compensation will also dip, since it is tied to overall performance. While this general accountability provides an incentive for the practice leader to ensure his or her practice's performance, it does not necessarily incentivise the practice leader to hold the new partner accountable for the business and development plans created at the outset of the hire. Nor does it force the practice leader to alter his or her behaviour. Instead of engaging the new lateral to pursue a new client opportunity, for example, the practice leader may turn to a longstanding partner who is a 'known entity' and seen as less risky. Without someone at the firm who is directly accountable for following up on the promises of a newcomer, these types of issues will snowball, with the likely result of a premature departure of what was once a promising – and expensive – lateral hire.

That said, the systems in place for partner hiring and accountability appear sophisticated compared to those for business professionals and associates. Since associates are most often hired for expertise and potential, rather than for their books of business, law firms generally do not have bright-line metrics (aside from hours) on which to assess their performance and hold the associates and hiring partners accountable for it. The business plan and accountability issues are even more pronounced for lateral business professionals. **Our research interviewees consistently noted that if a business case was created for the lateral business professional, it was generally not revisited for accountability purposes. Instead, it went in a file and stayed there.** As an executive at one large international firm described: "We certainly don't do the same level of involvement [for executive hires] that we would for a lateral partner. I mean, it's surprising, but true. And I think it's just managed a little bit differently. We tend to work through a process of the various chief officers recruiting different people at either the director level or associate director level and going through their review, and then other chiefs will be involved in kind of vetting that person. But it's just not as rigorous in my view as it would be, say, for a lateral partner."

Allowing such ambiguity with respect to performance objectives is a recipe for frustration and limited success. Consider using outside consultants to help define these measures.

To improve lateral success and hold stakeholders accountable, firms must do the following:

- Make it clear to hiring groups that their ability to hire future laterals will depend on how successfully they integrate each newcomer. You might not be able to measure immediate financial results, but you can track activity. For example, how many partners have used the newcomer's expertise to develop joint pitches or to create new intellectual property such as white papers? When partners do create these opportunities, celebrate them across the firm. Recognition for good behaviour not only encourages more partners to engage in it, but also helps to

spread the newcomer's reputation as a collaborative, value-adding asset within the firm.
- Set expectations that the integration process will be three to four years, and create goals for what is expected to happen in each of those years.
- Check in with the lateral hire with respect to his or her business plan, individual development plan and other agreed-upon metrics at three-month, six-month, nine-month and one-year intervals to identify and remedy issues before they escalate.

Most law firms need to become far better at setting and communicating specific objectives. For example, at the three, six and nine-month check-ins, and later in reviews, there is often no clarity around, "I need you to do A, B and C" or "I expect you to do X, Y and Z." Instead, the language is qualified or hedged – there are no bright lines. Interviewees suggest this practice is in place to provide the law firm with as much wiggle room as possible, possibly for fear of future lawsuits. We believe this is one area where law firms would do well to take a bit more 'risk', and clearly delineate and communicate objectives and expectations to employees and hold them accountable for the same.

3.6 Continuously audit and revamp the lateral integration process

As organisational behaviour expert Bill Torbert espoused in his classic and award-winning work, *Managing the Corporate Dream: Restructuring for Long-Term Success*: "as an organization matures, its identity becomes lodged less in its current structure than its capacity for restructuring to more consistently enact the corporate dream."[71] In other words, a maintenance or status quo mindset does not allow organisations to continue to develop and mature as required to thrive and reach evolving objectives. Firms need to schedule and trigger reflection points. In this reflection, the firm should question not only current processes, but also the underlying assumptions.

In considering how to change and customise your firm's lateral integration programme, start by auditing the effectiveness of current processes. The audit will help to measure the success of your current efforts and will also provide data for the business case justifying additional resources allocated to the process (see Table 9 for an 'off-the-rack' audit of current efforts and consider the four templates provided in the Appendix for continued development of your integration schedule).

Table 9. Survey questions to audit current partner integration procedures

Questions to ask lateral partners from past five years regarding their integration experiences
• How much interaction with other partners throughout the firm (either in person or via phone or video) did you have in the first three to six months? Was it enough to help you to integrate into client work and other value-adding activities? • With respect to collaborative client service, were you introduced to any firm clients during your first six months at the firm? • What resources (eg, people, department, online) did you find most helpful in your first 30 days with the firm? • What in your initial training/orientation was helpful? What was missing? • On a scale of 1 to 5, with 5 being the best, how would you rate the conflicts process with regard to transferring clients? • How smooth was the physical delivery and integration of your files from your previous firm? • Are there substantive issues that you feel have not been adequately communicated/explained to you properly prior to/since your arrival? If so, what are they?

Source: https://info.legalsolutions.thomsonreuters.com/signup/newsletters/practice-innovations/2016-oct/oct16_PracticeInnovations.pdf

IV. Conclusion

Many one-dimensional legal problems that, some years ago, a single practice expert could have solved have now matured into multi-faceted business problems that span departments, disciplines and jurisdictions. Lawyers are now expected to solve 'problem problems', rather than address purely legal issues. At the same time, the legal market is consolidating, facing fierce competition from both within and outside the profession. Law firms are facing unprecedented demands from clients to innovate not only on the legal solutions they provide, but also on how these are provided. Law firm executives are creating processes to respond to client demands, while also driving market share in a shrinking, highly competitive profession. The business of law has grown from simple partnerships with administrative support functions to large, multinational firms with affiliate networks and increasingly complex business structures. Law firm executives are now expected to solve 'business of law' problems. Accordingly, law firms are in a battle for talented lawyers and business professionals, with one prime talent objective across all: problem-solving power.

And the fight is on. Law firms, in-house legal departments, late-stage start-ups, premier consulting, financial and accounting firms – they are all circling and closing in to steal your best talent. You need that talent to maintain your firm's portfolio of cross-disciplinary expertise to solve both client problems and your firm's own business challenges. Compounding the actual service challenges, the costs of losing lateral hires can prove debilitating: beyond the financial costs, poor lateral hiring can lead to strain on internal resources, internal friction and strife related to unequal compensation, cultural dissonance and the weakening of client confidence, which all slash the bottom line.

So how do you retain your expensive lateral hires, ensure their productivity and ultimately enhance your firm's viability? Analyse your current efforts using the three-stage process for successful lateral hiring outlined in this special report and then recalibrate and build your programme to incorporate the best practices that align with your firm's strategic objectives. **The firms that get it right – that is, those that discover the talent mix that is aligned with the overall firm strategy and develop an effective plan to locate, lure and lock in that talent – will emerge the victors**.

Most law firms are currently misallocating their time, attention, personnel and financial resources in the hiring process. Typical firms devote nearly all their energy to interviewing and wooing candidates. This old-fashioned approach must be radically altered to favour the strategic preparation stage and the post-hire integration stage.

1. Preparing to hire

In Chapter III, Stage 1, we emphasised the importance of a basic prerequisite to your entire lateral hiring programme: you must first connect your talent plan to the firm-wide strategic plan. Talent is core to your firm's value proposition, not peripheral. From there, firms need to shift from reactive hiring to a deliberate, proactive, data-driven approach, and develop forecasting systems that help them to do so. A hiring strategy based on past or in-demand needs will not provide the agility necessary to outpace the competition. Admittedly, this is easier said than done. Most often, however, the challenge is that already over-burdened lawyers are tasked with, but not trained in, developing the firm-wide lateral hiring programme. In many firms, lateral programme chair positions are coveted as a leadership opportunity or status indicator, but the lawyer who gets appointed then dedicates a minimal proportion of time to the task. The oversight, development and augmentation of your entire talent strategy – in an organisation that literally competes on talent – deserves more than that. **Allocate the budget and hire a dedicated professional to strategically overhaul, then lead, your lateral hiring process. The investment will pay off.**

Once you have the infrastructure in place to give lateral hiring the appropriate attention and resources, map out your overall talent gaps and anticipated needs. For each, define the expertise needed and think creatively about the professional best suited to fill the gap. Consider

"Most firms currently spend about 15% of time on Stage 1, 80% on Stage 2 and only 5% on Stage 3. For success, firms instead need to spread their efforts more evenly across the three phases."

lateral hiring as an opportunity for a 'blue ocean strategy' – a new market where demand is created, rather than fought over, and ample opportunity exists for profitable and rapid growth.[72] Create the market. If you think you need an esteemed partner to chair your lateral partner programme, question your assumptions. Yes, you need someone to lead the process whose judgement is trusted by partners, and you certainly need multiple partners involved in various stages of the hiring process. Yet to run the lateral programme, an entrepreneurial professional with a legal background and talent development experience might prove highly effective, and no one else in the market may be thinking about this person for that role. You have created the demand for that professional.

But we are getting ahead of ourselves. Before you even look outside the firm for talent, set the bar high to convince yourself that a lateral is the only option. If so, pause. Do not run ahead until you have assessed your organisation's readiness to absorb the lateral and have created a robust, data-based business case for the lateral hire. In your assessments, consider the practice group or department that the lateral hire will join – what is its success rate with lateral hires? Are you hiring for a 'churn and burn' department or one with lifelong lateral loyalists? This type of reflection and labelling not only holds practice group leaders and department heads accountable, but also provides insight into the capabilities required for the lateral to be welcomed and productive within the new team, and how much time you will need to allocate to integrating the lateral to ensure his or her success. Include the identified capabilities in the job description and the estimates in the Stage 3 plan, along with the concrete objectives for the new role. Firms must make expectations clear at the outset so that they can hold themselves accountable for both measurable ROI and the ultimate satisfaction of the lateral hire.

Now that you have your business plan in support of a lateral hire and job description, the question becomes: where will you find the perfect person for the role? You likely have streams of talent already built, from partner referrals, recruiters or association job banks. As you pursue your talent strategy, however, you need to access much more than streams – you need robust, sprawling estuaries of diverse talent. Be careful not to overextend and dilute your efforts. Instead, build consensus on the capabilities needed to become or remain successful in the long term; decide where you want to place your bets. Then, implement a targeted and deliberate multi-pronged strategy to source and develop the suite of talent needed for your firm's ultimate success.

Before you begin interviewing, consider the support required for the lateral's success. Firms should review their business plan for the newcomer and match the support offered with the objectives for the role. A rainmaker will need a hefty marketing budget. C-level business executives will need firm-wide respect. Do all that you can to make that happen.

2. Recruiting and interviewing
Chapter III, Stage 2 delineated essential steps for optimisation, including the following:

- Search for capabilities over credentials.
- Identify and train the right group of people to conduct the interviews using behavioural-based techniques.
- Use the interview data to debrief and make decisions.
- Close the deal.

Firms first must understand the difference between capabilities (ability to do the job) and credentials (shiny CV highlights). Law firms are still stuck on being wooed by credentials – what sociologist Lauren Rivera calls 'pedigree' – even though this approach is generally misguided.[73] Firms often to succumb to credentials, such as membership of a law review, which turn out to be false clues and are often negative predictors of future performance. To ensure that your firm is properly interviewing for the desired capabilities and not succumbing to the lure of certain credentials, you must identify and train the right group of people to properly interview.

Firms can vastly improve lateral hiring by using multiple structured interviews to triangulate on technical and leadership competence, collaborative capacity (the ability to develop, work with and leverage networks), cultural and role fit, and firm experience. Zeroing in on these competencies requires that interviewers be assigned a specific competence to probe and be trained in conducting behavioural-based interviews to assess for that competence. To achieve this level of sophistication and data-driven hiring, the firm first must define the capabilities necessary for the role, as discussed above, to then interview for them. The interview process should then be structured into:

- behavioural interviews targeted at specific capabilities;
- qualification scores on specific metrics (eg, CV grading); and
- efficient and expedient interview debriefs.

Of all the research and data packed into this book, one of the most compelling arguments for our Stage 2 approach is the fact that improving the quality of assessments is:

- three times more profitable than increasing the size of the candidate pool; and
- six times more profitable than getting the chosen candidate to accept a lower compensation package.[74]

In the war for talent, this news is encouraging. It means that you likely have great candidates already coming through your doors. The trick is to do a better job identifying and capturing them in a timely manner. Remember, the experience that lateral candidates have in interviewing at your firm will leave a lasting impression on them that they will likely share with others in the market for talent, and perhaps even with clients. It directly affects your reputation – a critical asset to proactively manage and protect.

3. Integration

In Chapter III, Stage 3 we showed how strong integration programmes address potential challenges upfront. Successful firms view full integration as a long-term process that requires structure, feedback and commitment from both the firm and the new recruit. In other professions, formal integration begins before the new hire's start dates and continues for six months, with check-ins and training at regular intervals. The overarching goals of integration revolve around making the lateral hire feel welcomed and getting the lateral up to speed technically and culturally so that he or she can hit the ground running. Take advantage of the 'honeymoon period', when the hire is eager to sample the firm's opportunities and still energised by the newness of it all, to shape positive impressions all around. Develop entry processes to help the new joiner find ways to authentically offer his or her unique contributions to colleagues in ways that they will value. As we learned from Professor Rob Cross's research,[75] new hires need networks that jumpstart productivity and inclusion in their first year; while in Years 2 to 5, employees need networks that drive collaborative efficiency and generate a sense of purpose in their work. Assigning a variety of mentors who can help the hire to build internal and external networks and become productive quickly is a great start, but it does not stop there. Your social capital strategy must evolve with the needs of the lateral hire – as with most things in life, these needs are not static.

One thing that should remain fixed in this process is accountability. It is critical. Firms need concrete plans against which they can measure performance, and these plans should identify the person who is directly accountable for the lateral's success or failure. Without clear accountability and follow-up on the promises of and to the new lateral, small issues will escalate and you will lose your highly sought-after lateral hire. All of that work – conducting strategic meetings, drafting business plans, analysing talent needs and success rates across departments and groups, developing the talent pool and allocating the necessary support, gaining consensus on the capabilities required, training the right people to interview the right way, debriefing to make decisions, closing the deal, formally integrating the new hire, assigning peer mentors and creating individual development plans – all of it for naught. That is not a winning business strategy.

A status quo mindset is also not a winning strategy in the legal profession, which increasingly feels as though it is resting on a fault line, enduring tremors and just hoping the Magnitude 10 earthquake will not hit. Firms must schedule and trigger reflection points where they question fundamental assumptions about their talent strategy, and develop and test new processes or practices in an effort to meet ever-evolving objectives. These reflection points should occur regularly, not just annually.

Our call to action is to harness the full power of your talent and engage your lateral hires, along with incumbents, in smart collaboration. Now is the time for research-based, strategic change to successfully recruit and integrate laterals in law firms.

Appendix

Lateral hiring toolkit for law firms

Law firms have vastly different levels of sophistication when it comes to analysing lateral hiring data. Some firms are highly active in the lateral market and have amassed and reviewed their data, while others are just starting to think about the process. Across the board, however, analyses tend to be limited to the fundamentals – for example, whether the firm has more success in hiring lateral solos or cohorts. Ample opportunity exists for more robust analyses, including those that incorporate accountability measures such as tracking pockets of churn and burn across groups. The good news is that nearly all firms have the data; their effectiveness hinges on organising and analysing it effectively to produce actionable insights. We have designed this toolkit with varying levels of sophistication in mind and encourage you to adapt it over time as your needs evolve.

For additional instructions and to download some of these tools, visit www.heidikgardner.com or www.anusiagillespie.com.

Tool 1: Analysing lateral hire success to find pockets of excellence and opportunities for improvement

This tool is designed to help you to:

- understand which factors most affect lateral hires' success (or lack thereof) at your firm;
- locate the pockets of success (eg, practice groups, offices, individual hiring partners) so that you can see what approaches they use, replicate them elsewhere and reward these high-performing groups (eg, by granting them more resources for hiring); and
- uncover areas or individuals with a poor track record in lateral hiring so that you can coach them and ensure that these poorly performing groups do not waste lateral hiring resources that are unlikely to be successful until they change their approach.

To help guide you through this tool, we have broken down the process into three steps.

Step 1: gather the data

Input all lateral hire information from the last five years, with a specific focus on who pushed for or sponsored the request, and how well each of those laterals performed once hired. The sources of this data will vary from firm to firm, but in general you might be able to pull these numbers from HR files which track basic personnel data, performance management databases and billing and timesheet records, to understand who has worked with whom and how integrated hires are with deals/cases/ projects.

Be as specific as possible; accuracy garners the best results. Focus solely on gathering the data at this point. Wait to look for insights in Step 2.

Lateral hiring process					Original role		Current role			Accountability leader	Overall performance			Final insights
Start Date	Name	Employment status	Cohort or solo hire	Referring sponsor	Title	Department	Title	Department	Promoted (Y/N)	Name	Overall performance	Progress v business case	Integration & collaboration	

Step 2: analyse your data

Use the chart below to think through the types of questions and insights specific to each category. Review your data with an analytical approach. A basic strategy is to sort by category in an Excel spreadsheet to quickly reveal patterns. More advanced analysts can use statistical approaches such as correlations to unearth patterns that are less apparent. Try visualising the data in various ways, for example over time, to see trends.

Category	Questions and insights
Start date	• Consider the impact of timing (eg, economy) on lateral hiring success.
Employment status	• Has the lateral hire been voluntarily or involuntarily terminated? Or is he or she still an active employee of the firm? • Are the majority of your lateral hires still working at the firm? If not, consider why.
Cohort or solo hire	• Does a solo or cohort hire affect the likelihood of long-term success? • Were lateral hire outcomes similar across a cohort? • Were there any outliers? If so, consider why.
Lateral hire's sponsor	• Name the individual who recommended the lateral hire to the firm. • Do certain firm leaders have a better track record for selecting top lateral hiring talent than others? • Alternatively, look for sponsors who recommend lateral hires but fail to provide the support required for the laterals' success.
Original versus current title and department	• Identify whether the lateral hire remained in the same role and department or transferred elsewhere. • For associates, a change in title or department may indicate excellent performance, as top talent often move throughout the firm. But test this assumption: such a pattern might also indicate that someone is having trouble finding their niche. • Look carefully to see whether certain departments have higher-than-expected switching patterns, which may reveal that laterals are under-supported in those departments. • Pay special attention to the departments that laterals are flocking to and fleeing from. • Promotion rates are very important (eg, associate to partner; income to equity partner; director to chief).
Accountability leader	• Who is responsible and accountable for the lateral's continued success? • Review 'employment status' to determine levels of churn connected to poor leadership. Who is poor and who is great?

continued on next page

Category	Questions and insights
Overall performance	• Based on metrics consistently used and accepted by your firm, how has this lateral hire performed? • Compared to the business case that the lateral hire and his or her department put forward, how has performance emerged? • How well integrated was the lateral hire? Specifically, did colleagues involve the lateral on client deals or matters? And did the lateral hire generate work that he or she brought others into? • Consider how involved the hiring sponsor is in the lateral's integration after joining the firm. Involvement can be analysed by the number of client introductions initiated, regular follow-up and feedback sessions, and general networking introductions made among colleagues.
Overall insights	• After controlling for the metrics in the table, consider what your key takeaways are for each lateral. • By compiling each data point, firms can better indicate trends across the board.

Step 3: generate insights

We have compiled some illustrative data to show you exactly how to make meaningful connections from the data collected. For ease and clarity, some categories have been left intentionally empty to direct your attention to another specific metric. In this case, the data is collected from three departments: tax, real estate and data privacy. After reviewing Step 3 carefully, return to your data to look for additional insights.

Lateral hiring process					Original role		Current role			Accountability leader	Overall performance			Final insights
Start Date	Name	Employment status	Cohort or solo hire	Referring sponsor	Title	Department	Title	Department	Promoted (Y/N)	Name	Overall performance	Progress v business case	Integration & collaboration	
05-Sep-13	Eliza Sanchez	active	solo		Associate	Tax	Senior associate	Tax	Y	Rick Shurette				3 lateral hires in the Tax department have left the firm, 1 transferred departments and 1 got promoted. That's a big problem! A follow up with Rick Shurette is required.
01-Dec-14	John Dunn	voluntarily terminated	solo		Partner	Tax				Rick Shurette				
15-Jan-15	Chris Shay	involuntarily terminated	solo		Senior associate	Tax				Rick Shurette				
10-Mar-15	Marge Little	active	solo		Associate	Tax	Senior associate	Data privacy group	N	Rick Shurette				
22-Mar-16	Joel Camp	voluntarily terminated	solo		Partner	Tax				Rick Shurette				
12-Oct-14	Amber Reynolds	active	solo		Senior associate	Real estate				April O'Connor				At first glance, the Real Estate group appears to be a mixed bag. But closer analysis reveals that the laterals reporting to April O'Connor are still at the firm! Joe Salucci should find out what April is doing right.
21-Jun-13	Joseph Parker	voluntarily terminated	solo		Partner	Real estate				Joe Salucci				
06-Jan-15	Jonah Doner	active	solo		Partner	Real estate				April O'Connor				
01-Feb-15	Jane Dorset	voluntarily terminated	cohort		Partner	Real estate				Joe Salucci				
01-Feb-15	Bill Young	voluntarily terminated	cohort		Associate	Real estate				Joe Salucci				
01-May-15	Kate Schu-bert	active	cohort		Senior associate	Data privacy				Bob Clark				Bob Clark has kept all three lateral hires. Go, Bob. Rick should talk to Bob to find out what strategies he's utilising to help his lateral hires thrive.
01-May-15	Michael Flay	active	cohort		Partner	Data privacy				Bob Clark				
01-May-15	Melanie Jones	active	cohort		Senior associate	Data privacy				Bob Clark				

Tool 2: Strategy checklist

Use the checklist below as a starting point to create a customised strategy checklist, with questions to answer before deciding whether, when, where and what profile to hire.

	Strategy checklist	
	Item	**Completed by (who and when)**
Whether to hire externally	The position supports our firm-wide, long-term strategy	
	We have a data-driven business plan for this hire	
	The position was posted on our internal job board	
	We have had conversations with at least three internal people who might be interested in and fit the position	
	Leaders agree that we need to hire laterally and are willing to provide resources to promote the newcomer's success	
When	We have designated someone senior in the firm who is accountable for the success of this hire	
	We have set a target for the hire's start date	
	We have processes in place to recruit a lateral hire and position the hire for success by that start date	
Where	We have considered various office locations for the placement of the new hire	
	The office location we chose is prepared to integrate a lateral hire	
Who	We have decided whether the lateral hire must be a lawyer	
	We have defined the capabilities, beyond technical competence, that the hire must possess	
	We have committed to interviewing at least 50% diverse candidates	

Tool 3: Decision tree to answer the threshold question of whether the firm should hire

As priorities, personnel or client projects shift, firms may need to continually reassess whether a lateral hire fits into the overall firm strategy. This decision tree is designed to help guide firm leadership through this process by answering simple 'yes' and 'no' prompts.

Lateral hiring

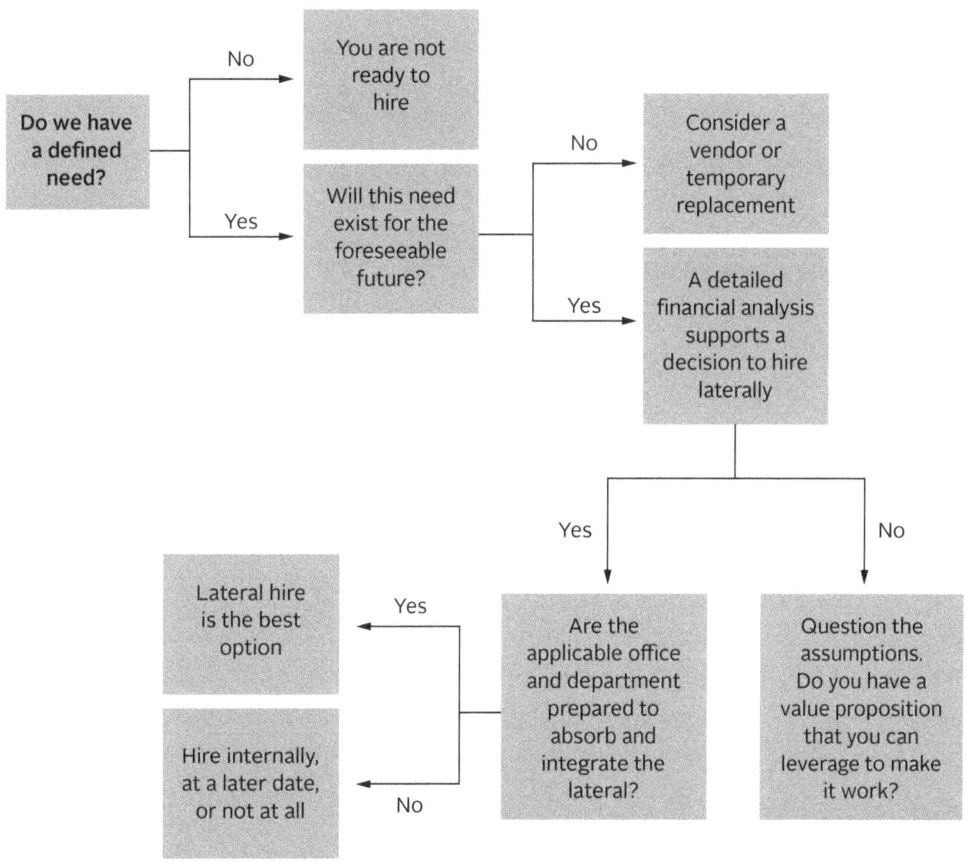

Tool 4: Financial *pro forma* to answer the threshold question of whether the firm should hire

Build a template *pro forma* for each type of hire – partner, business professional and associate. Use the three-year *pro forma* below as a starting point to develop your templates. The tool is broken into four parts:

- value of hire;
- hiring and integration costs;
- compensation; and
- possible three-year payout.

You will note that in this example, the 'conservative' scenario projects a loss of almost $295,400. This figure is very close to the average payout of lateral hires for a 12-year period in one AmLaw 100 firm that we studied (when accounting for each person's fully loaded overhead).

Value of hire assumptions

The interviewing candidate claims a book of business of $800,000 in annual revenue. Most research suggests that it takes about three years (or more) for laterally hired partners to match the revenue achieved at their old firm – if they succeed, that is. As such, we have included this assumption by providing a confidence level range (conservative – optimistic) to more accurately forecast revenue. Revenue estimates were based on what chief financial officers in our research thought lateral hires could produce in their first year (40%–60%), second year (50%–70%), and third year (70%–100%).

- We recommend using real data from each department about the likelihood of success in your firm to increase accuracy. And return to Tool 1 to discover pockets of excellence and failure within practice groups and across the firm.
- Goodwill: Some firms may, at least mentally, account for goodwill, which is an intangible asset that is essentially a quantified measure of reputation. To make the numbers less subjective, however, we recommend including only actual costs and revenues.

Hiring and integration cost assumptions

The costs of hiring laterals vary between firms, in part according to the number of incumbent partners and staff involved in the hiring and integration process. Be sure to reference your firm's historical data to ensure proper forecasting.

- We recommend using the concept of 'opportunity costs' to calculate the expense associated with interviewing lateral candidates. The advantage to using this approach is that it is easy and simple to calculate. Be careful not to overinflate the costs of non-legal business professionals who serve as interviewers, as they do not have a billing rate.

- For simplicity, imagine that all of the partners involved in interviewing have the same billing rates, compensation and so forth. If each partner has a billing rate of $800 per hour and each candidate is interviewed by seven partners for one hour each, then allocate ($800/hour × 7 hours) = $5,600 per candidate for partner interviewing costs.

In our model, compensation over three years for laterally hired partners remained flat in years when they did not reach their full projected (claimed) revenue levels. Compensation could increase if the laterally hired partner achieves success more quickly due to effective integration practices.

- Note that this model does not account for fully loaded personnel costs – merely compensation. If your firm has accurate data, we encourage you to include it in your analysis.

Three-year financial *pro forma* for lateral hire

	Conservative Estimate	Optimistic Estimate
Value of hire (claimed portable book of business = $800,000)		
Anticipated revenue in year 1 (at 40%–60% confidence level)	$320,000	$480,000
Anticipated revenue in year 1 (at 50%–80% confidence level)	$400,000	$640,000
Anticipated revenue in year 2 (at 70%–100% confidence level)	$560,000	$800,000
Goodwill with market (external reputation)	$0	$200,000
Total value	**$1,280,000**	**$2,120,000**
Hiring & integration: partner opportunity costs		
Preparing to hire (4-8 hours developing & reviewing a business plan)	$6,400	$3,200
Recruiting & negotiating (10-20 hours spent by partners)	$16,000	$8,000
Interviewing (5 to 15 one-hour, partner-level interviews)	$12,000	$4,000
Integration (5-20 hours of training, coaching and mentoring provided by incumbent partners for smooth transition)	$16,000	$4,000
Compensation		
Compensation in Year 1	$500,000	$500,000
Compensation in Year 2	$500,000	$500,000
Compensation in Year 3	$525,000	$500,000
Total investment (with successful integration)	**$1,575,400**	**$1,519,200**
Possible 3-year payout (Total value – total investment)	**($295,400)**	**$600,800**

Tool 5: Interview form

Consider creating interview forms tailored to the open position. Provide these forms to interviewers to use as a guide. Include behaviour-based questions, targeting specific competencies required for the position, and a scoring component. Require interviewers to submit the form the same day as the interview. Use the template below as a starting point.

Sophisticated interviewers seek candidates with strong collaborative competencies. Specifically, look for individuals who demonstrate these qualities (listed below) throughout the interview process by asking behavioural probing questions such as those in the table.

- Adaptability
- Conflict management
- Initiative and follow-through
- Integrity
- Learning motivation/curiosity
- Listening and probing
- Networking
- Perseverance
- Persuasiveness (leading without authority)
- Political sensitivity

Overall opinion

Not qualified Impressed

1 2 3 4 5 6 7 8 9 10

Questions	Comments
Collaborative	
• Tell me about a situation when you teamed up with colleagues to solve a really tough client problem. • Follow-on: How did you find the right experts? How did you know they were capable? How did you convince them to join the effort? What role did you play after the team was formed? • Describe a time when you needed a colleague's input on client work, but that person did not respond to requests. What did you do? Give me an example of a time when you uncovered an opportunity to serve a client with a multi-practice team. What ultimately happened?	
Leadership	
Describe a time you faced a conflict with a partner – what was this issue and what did you do?	
Communication	
Tell me about a time you had to deliver constructive feedback to a co-worker. How did you do it? What was the other person's reaction? Tell me about a time you found it difficult to negotiate with a sponsor/stakeholder. What did you do?	
Willingness to learn	
What was the last training you attended? How did you use your new knowledge in practice?	
Operational/situational	
When having to undertake multiple projects, how do you prioritise them?	
Behavioural	

Tool 6: The what, why and when of integration[1]

This tool lays out how the timing and purpose of each integration tool is woven together to create a seamless integration experience for lateral hires. Forward-thinking firms ensure that the integration process is clearly communicated to all departments involved – IT, HR, the hiring department and firm leadership – and that the necessary buy-in is secured.

How should you use this tool?

Review your firm's current integration process against the best practices in the chart below. What are the similarities and differences in timing, departmental responsibilities and breadth of experience? Consider the impact of incorporating one (or more) new integration practice into your firm's established process. Perhaps transform this tool into a worksheet by adding the responsible party and personalising to each lateral hire.

1 *Source: Adapted from TN Bauer and E Elder, "Integrating newcomers into organizations", presentation at the Society for Human Resource Management Annual Conference, Washington DC (2006); JA Conger and B Fishel, "Accelerating leadership performance at the top: Lessons from the Bank of America's executive on-boarding process",* Human Resource Management Review, *17, 442–454, Case Study: Executive Integration at Bank of America (p14) (2007).*

Integration tool	Why is it used?	When is it used?
Welcome packet	To 'put a face to the name' through informational material and formally welcome the new executive to the firm.	Sent after acceptance of offer
Online portal	Provides HR and other technical, logistical or compliance training.	One month before start date
Email address created	Begins cultural assimilation.	Two weeks before start date
Orientation programme	Includes information on the business, history, culture and values of the firm. (This is NOT 'a day with HR').	First day on the job
Written integration plan	Helps new executives to organise and prioritise the integration process.	Sponsor creates the initial draft before the new hire's first day on the job. The newcomer creates his or hers during the first week after entry
Leadership tools	Help new executives to understand the leadership frameworks at the firm (ie, what is valued).	First week after entry
Key stakeholder meetings	Allow for important flows of information and for expectation setting.	Must be done in the first two months
New peer integration	Helps to accelerate the development of relationships between the new executive and the rest of the executive team.	Occurs between two and three months after entry
Key stakeholder check-in meetings	Helps to diagnose potential problems, receive development feedback and create solutions.	Monthly for the first half year
Executive networking forums	Help new executives to connect and network with other executives.	Held quarterly
360-degree feedback	Helps new executives to gauge how they are performing on key metrics as measured by those around them.	Occurs six months after entry

Notes

1 Heidi K Gardner, *Smart Collaboration: How Professionals and Their Firms Succeed by Breaking Down Silos*, Harvard Business Review Press, 2017.
2 Boris Groysberg, Ashish Nanda and Nitin Nohria, "The Risky Business of Hiring Stars", *Harvard Business Review*, 1 August 2014, hbr.org/2004/05/the-risky-business-of-hiring-stars.
3 R Cross, *et al, Connect and adapt* (Organ Dyn, 2017), http://dx.doi.org/10.1016/j.orgdyn.2017.08.003.
4 "Lateral Damage: Failed Hires Cost London Dear," *The Lawyer*, February 2012.
5 Hugh A Simons, "Global Lateral Hiring by The Numbers: A Look Behind the High 5-Year Attrition Rate", *The American Lawyer International*, 3 February 2017. This finding is based on an examination of where the 1,130 partners hired laterally by the 100 highest profit per equity partner AmLaw 200 firms in 2011 were practising at the end of 2016. The laterals examined are those identified by ALM Rival Edge and include both equity and non-equity partners. US laterals comprise 70% of the total.
6 Boushey, Heather & Glynn, Sarah James, *Cost of losing talent*, Center American Progress, 2012.
7 The Law Society (UK), *Private Practice Solicitor Salaries 2016*; Jonathan Prynn, "Average pay for top partners at London law firm Linklaters smashes £1.5 million", *London Evening Standard*, 30 June 2017.
8 Matthew Bidwell, "Paying More to Get Less: The Effects of External Hiring versus Internal Mobility", *Administrative Science Quarterly*, September 2011 vol 56 no 3 369–407.
9 www.wisnik.com/wp-content/uploads/2013/11/Wisnik-Marketing_BD-Salary-Survey-2013.pdf.
10 Joan Williams and Cynthia Thomas Calvert, Project for Attorney Retention Final Report, 2001.
11 R Cross, *et al, Connect and adapt* (Organ Dyn, 2017).
12 www.forbes.com/sites/kimberlywhitler/2011/10/04/the-disposable-cmo-the-downside-of-high-cmo-turnover/#59b704723520.
13 Based on survey responses from 68 law firms, which included 22% of the world's top 50 law firms.
14 www.forbes.com/sites/kimberlywhitler/2011/10/04/the-disposable-cmo-the-downside-of-high-cmo-turnover/#59b704723520.
15 www.nytimes.com/2017/09/22/business/dealbook/pwc-law-firm-ilc.html.
16 Hugh A Simons and Gina Passarella, "The Rise (and Fall?) of In-House Counsel", *The American Lawyer*, 25 February 2018, www.law.com/americanlawyer/2018/02/25/the-rise-and-fall-of-in-house-counsel/.
17 https://workforceinstitute.org/onboarding-process/.
18 TN Bauer, T Bodner, B Erdogan, DM Truxillo and JS Tucker (2007), "Newcomer adjustment during organizational socialization: A meta-analytic review of antecedents, outcomes and methods", *Journal of Applied Psychology*, 92, 707-721; DM Cable and CK Parsons, "20 Socialization tactics and person-organization fit", *Personnel Psychology*, 54, 1-23 (2001); T Kim, DM Cable and S Kim, "Socialization tactics, employee proactivity, and person-organization fit", *Journal of Applied Psychology*, 90, 232-241 (2005); AM Saks, KL Uggerslev and NE Fassina (2007), "Socialization tactics and newcomer adjustment: A meta-analytic review and test of a model", *Journal of Vocational Behavior*, 70, 413-446.
19 www.shrm.org/resourcesandtools/hr-topics/talent-acquisition/pages/new-employee-onboarding-guide.aspx.
20 Our analyses are described by researchers as a 'conservative test' because only statistically significant findings from across multiple firms are reported. Partners in two firms outside our dataset – one law and one accounting firm – explained that analyses of their own firms' data revealed that the critical window for achieving collaboration is as short as six months after a laterally hired partner joins their firm.
21 Rob Cross, *et al, Connect and adapt* (Organ Dyn, 2017).
22 www.robcross.org/wp-content/uploads/2017/05/connect-and-adapt-improving-retention-and-engagement-in-first-five-years.pdf.
23 Michael Porter, "What Is Strategy?", *Harvard Business Review*, Nov–Dec 1996.
24 Professor John Coates, Harvard Law School.
25 Jay Lorsch and Tom Tierney, *Aligning the Stars: How to Succeed When Professionals Drive Results*, Harvard Business Review Press, 2002.
26 Heidi K Gardner, "Hiring Successful Professionals: One Process – Multiple Goals," *Background Note*, Harvard Business School Case Collection, July 2010
27 Boris Groysberg, Nitin Nohria and Claudio Fernandez-Araoz, "The Definitive Guide to Recruiting in Good Times and Bad", *Harvard Business Review*, May 2009.
28 Confidential interview with the US-based COO of an international consulting firm.
29 Hugh A Simons, "Global Lateral Hiring by The Numbers: A Look Behind the High 5-Year Attrition Rate", *The American Lawyer International*, 3 February 2017.
30 www.orrick.com/Innovation/Orrick-Labs.
31 Richard Susskind, *Tomorrow's Lawyers: An Introduction to Your Future*, Oxford University Press, 2013.
32 www.law.com/legaltechnews/sites/legaltechnews/2017/10/10/richard-susskind-on-artificial-intelligence/.
33 Corporate Legal Operations Consortium, http://cloc.org/.
34 "The Impact of Job Referrals: Effects on Pay, Engagement, Diversity", white paper by Payscale, www.payscale.com/content/whitepaper/wp_ImpactofJobReferrals.pdf?_ga=2.182852262.18703023 42.1522408094-1926370411.1522408094.

35 "The Impact of Job Referrals: Effects on Pay, Engagement, Diversity", white paper by Payscale, www.payscale.com/content/whitepaper/wp_ImpactofJobReferrals.pdf?_ga=2.182852262.18703023 42.1522408094-1926370411.1522408094.
36 https://hbr.org/2018/03/how-to-use-employee-referrals-without-giving-up-workplace-diversity.
37 https://blogs.wsj.com/digits/2015/08/03/intel-doubles-up-on-hiring-women-and-minorities/.
38 www.eeoc.gov/laws/practices/.
39 "Coping with the talent shortage: How GE, Rochester and other US firms have approached the recruitment conundrum", *Human Resource Management International Digest*, Bradford: 2007. Vol 15, Iss 3; p6.
40 www.careers-in-business.com/consulting/mcfacts.htm.
41 http://onrampfellowship.com/.
42 Boris Groysberg, *Chasing Stars: The Myth of Talent and the Portability of Performance* (Princeton University Press, 2010), p137.
43 Lauren A Rivera, *Pedigree: How Elite Students Get Elite Jobs* (2015, Print).
44 William Henderson, "Human Capital Accounting", www.billhenderson.com/articles/2014/9/1/human-capital-accounting.
45 http://fortune.com/2014/11/13/jc-penney-ron-johnson-ceo-succession/.
46 Boris Groysberg, Nitin Nohria and Claudio Fernandez-Araoz, "The Definitive Guide to Recruiting in Good Times and Bad", *Harvard Business Review*, May 2009.
47 Heidi Gardner, *Smart Collaboration: How Professionals and Their Firms Succeed by Breaking Down Silos* (Harvard Business Review Press), pp53–55.
48 https://hbr.org/2015/07/recruiting-for-cultural-fit.
49 Lauren Rivera, *Hiring As Cultural Matching*, p1017.
50 Lauren Rivera, *Hiring As Cultural Matching*, pp1017–18.
51 Lauren Rivera, *Hiring As Cultural Matching*, pp1017–18.
52 Lauren Rivera, *Hiring As Cultural Matching*, p1009.
53 Lauren Rivera, *Hiring As Cultural Matching*, p1009.
54 Denise M Rousseau, "Psychological and Implied Contracts in Organizations", *Employee Responsibilities and Rights Journal*, Vol 2, No 2, 1989.
55 The chart shows the lateral hiring rate (ie, the number of laterally hired partners as a percentage of total partners at hiring firms), and the five-year attrition rate, for firms organised by deciles of profitability (ie, decile 1 comprises the top 10% of firms by profits per partner, etc). Hugh A Simons, "Global Lateral Hiring by The Numbers: A Look Behind the High 5-Year Attrition Rate", *The American Lawyer International*, 3 February 2017.
56 Professor David Wilkins, Harvard Law School, personal communication with authors.
57 Don Moore, http://journals.sagepub.com/doi/full/10.1177/0008125617725288.
58 Iris Bohnet, "How to Take the Bias Out of Interviews", *Harvard Business Review*, 18 April 2016, https://hbr.org/2016/04/how-to-take-the-bias-out-of-interviews.
59 http://journals.sagepub.com/doi/full/10.1177/0008125617725288.
60 http://journals.sagepub.com/doi/full/10.1177/0008125617725288.
61 "Corporate Recruiters Get Inside the Interview", newsletter of the Graduate Management Admission Council, July 2012, www.gmac.com/why-gmac/gmac-news/gmnews/2012/july-2012/corporate-recruiters-get-inside-the-interview.aspx.
62 Don Moore, "How to Improve the Accuracy and Reduce the Cost of Personnel Selection", *California Management Review*, Vol 60(1) 8–17, 2017.
63 Boris Groysberg, "The Definitive Guide to Recruiting in Good Times and Bad", *Harvard Business Review*, May 2009.
64 https://blog.capabiliti.co/employee-onboarding-facebook-google-apple/.
65 Heidi Gardner, "Hiring successful Professionals: One Process – Multiple Goals", *Harvard Business Review*, 2010.
66 HBS case study, "Marketing at Wachtell, Lipton, Rosen & Katz," 9-496-037, p3.
67 Dan Cable, Francesca Gino, Bradley Staats, "The Powerful Way Onboarding Can Encourage Authenticity", 2015, https://hbr.org/2015/11/the-powerful-way-onboarding-can-encourage-authenticity.
68 Dan Cable, Francesca Gino, Bradley Staats, "The Powerful Way Onboarding Can Encourage Authenticity", 2015, https://hbr.org/2015/11/the-powerful-way-onboarding-can-encourage-authenticity.
69 R Cross, *et al, Connect and adapt* (Organ Dyn, 2017).
70 R Cross, *et al, Connect and adapt* (Organ Dyn, 2017).
71 William Torbert, *Managing the Corporate Dream.*
72 https://hbr.org/2004/10/blue-ocean-strategy.
73 Lauren A Rivera, *Pedigree: How Elite Students Get Elite Jobs* (2015, Print).
74 Boris Groysberg, "The Definitive Guide to Recruiting in Good Times and Bad", *Harvard Business Review*, May 2009.
75 R Cross, *et al, Connect and adapt* (Organ Dyn, 2017).

About the authors

Heidi K Gardner
Distinguished fellow at Harvard Law School's
Center on the Legal Profession
hgardner@law.harvard.edu

Heidi K Gardner, PhD, is a distinguished fellow at Harvard Law School's Center on the Legal Profession and faculty chair of the school's Accelerated Leadership Programme and other executive education courses. Previously she was a professor at Harvard Business School. Dr Gardner's book Smart Collaboration: How Professionals and Their Firms Succeed by Breaking Down Silos was published in 2017 by Harvard Business Press and became a Washington Post bestseller.

Dr Gardner's research received the Academy of Management's prize for Paper with Outstanding Practical Implications for Management. She has authored or co-authored more than 60 books, book chapters, case studies and articles in scholarly and practitioner journals, including multiple articles in Harvard Business Review. Her first book, Leadership for Lawyers: Essential Strategies for Law Firm Success (Globe Law and Business), was published in 2015. She has also been awarded an International Research Fellowship by Oxford University's Said Business School.

Dr Gardner has lived and worked on four continents, including as a Fulbright fellow, and for McKinsey & Co and Procter & Gamble. She earned her BA in Japanese from the University of Pennsylvania (summa cum laude, Phi Beta Kappa), a master's degree from the London School of Economics and a second master's and her PhD from London Business School. She was recently named by Thinkers 50 as a Next Generation Business Guru.

Her first book (co-edited with Rebecca Normand Hochman), *Leadership for Lawyers: Essential Strategies for Law Firm Success* (Globe Law and Business) was published in 2015, and the second edition will be released in 2019.

Anusia E Gillespie
Director of innovation, Eversheds Sutherland (US) LLP
anusiagillespie@eversheds-sutherland.com

Anusia E Gillespie is the director of innovation at Eversheds Sutherland (US) LLP, a global top 15 law firm with 66 offices in 32 countries.

Ms Gillespie has been studying and immersed in the business of law for over 10 years in a variety of capacities, including practice and business roles at law firms. She joined Eversheds Sutherland from Harvard Law School Executive Education, where she designed and developed business of law programmes for lawyers from around the world. While at Harvard Law, Ms Gillespie collaborated with Dr Gardner to undertake extensive research and interviews on lateral hiring in law firms in anticipation of this special report.

Ms Gillespie earned her bachelor of science in management from Tulane University's AB Freeman School of Business, her juris doctor from Boston College Law School and her master of business administration from Boston College Carroll Graduate School of Management. She was awarded a seat on BC Law's academic law journal, the Uniform Commercial Code Reporter Digest, and inducted into the Beta Gamma Honors Society, recognising honours in her graduate business studies.

About Globe Law and Business

Globe Law and Business was established in 2005 as an imprint of Globe Business Media Group. We set out to create law books which are sufficiently high level to be of real use to the experienced professional, yet still accessible and easy to navigate. Most of our authors are drawn from Magic Circle and other top commercial firms, both in the UK and internationally.

In Autumn 2015, we had an exciting turn in our history when Globe Law and Business was bought by a management team which includes my colleague Jim Smith and me, Sian O'Neill.

We love books, and our hardback titles are carefully produced, with the utmost attention paid to the editorial, design and production processes. We hope this results in high-quality titles which are easy to read, and a pleasure to own.

Our customers and authors are of paramount importance – we are committed to devoting time and attention to each book as well as everyone involved in the publishing process.

We'd very much like to hear from you with your thoughts on our titles or ideas for improving what we offer. Please do feel free to email me on sian@globelawandbusiness.com with your views.

Sian O'Neill, managing director

www.ingramcontent.com/pod-product-compliance
Ingram Content Group UK Ltd.
Pitfield, Milton Keynes, MK11 3LW, UK
UKHW052304040925
462600UK00005B/75

9 781787 421967